Stop Harming Customers

Stop Harming Customers

A Compliance Manifesto

David Silverman

BEP

BUSINESS EXPERT PRESS

Leader in applied, concise business books

First published in 2023 by
Business Expert Press, LLC
222 East 46th Street, New York, NY 10017
www.businessexpertpress.com

ISBN-13: 978-1-63742-539-8 (paperback)
ISBN-13: 978-1-63742-540-4 (e-book)

Business Expert Press Business Law and Corporate Risk Management Collection

First edition: 2023

10 9 8 7 6 5 4 3 2 1

Description

Since the year 2000, banks have been fined almost a third of a trillion dollars. Yet, every year billions more are imposed. Why? This book explains why banks break the law (it's not just the money), explains the challenges facing Compliance functions, considers that the majority of financiers don't want to do wrong, and puts forth a proposal to stop banks from harming customers.

The lessons in this book are applicable to any business where profit motives can conflict with customer benefit—in short, every business. (And if you're interested in cryptocurrency, this book is for you too!)

Keywords

compliance; management; risk; operational risk; reputation; fines; penalties; enforcement; violations; law; financial crime; white collar crime; fraud; regulations; regulators; banks; banking; finance; financial firm; Madoff; housing crisis; 2007 crisis; 2008 crisis; LIBOR; mortgage scandal; mortgage crisis; scandal; unfair; deceptive; money laundering; cryptocurrency; bitcoin; RCSA; control; assessment; testing; regulatory change; OCC; Comptroller of the Currency; Fed; CFPB; Federal Reserve; SEC; FINRA; CBOE; FDIC; Department of Justice; DOJ; Department of Treasury; FinCEN; FATF; Dodd–Frank; letter regulation; Reg E; Reg O; Reg P; Reg W; Reg Z; Reg GG; Gramm-Leach Bliley; fair credit; fair housing

Contents

Testimonials

"A Compliance book that answers both questions that are frequently asked in the Compliance world as well as the ones that you think don't have an answer. The only Compliance book I know of that is both informative and entertaining, I recommend it unreservedly."—**Juno Mayer-Senft, Legal and Compliance Consultant, Former Senior Compliance Leadership roles at JP Morgan, Bank of America and Merrill Lynch & Co**

"Written from the perspective of an industry insider, David Silverman provides an insightful, highly readable and amusing summary of the complex regulatory landscape in the US. I enjoyed this book immensely, learned a few things and highly recommend it to both the general public as well as the regulatory community."—**Mary Cvengros, Senior Fraud and Investigative Counsel United States Small Business Administration**

"David Silverman's book on complex topics of fiscal compliance and risk is not your typical business book. He approaches his topic with the knowledge of an industry insider but with wit and humor, making this a truly readable and enjoyable book. Silverman knows 'finance, like plumbing, is boring. Sooo boring. Put your head down on your desk and roll your eyes at even having to think about banking. Go ahead. It's important. I'll wait.' He unveils the hidden side of finance that we all pay for and tells us '$339,976,074,213... It's the amount of penalties paid by financial institutions between 2000 and July 2022.' Standing between the behemoth banks and the customer is 'a thin line of Compliance and Legal people inside the system' who need a more knowledgeable public who is aware of the harm caused to them. This is a book that seeks to awaken that public."—**Richard Greenwald, Dean of the College of Arts and Sciences and Professor of History at Fairfield University**

"Do no harm may be the axiom adopted by physicians globally, but the notion of Stop Harming Customers *is equally compelling. Through important case studies, informed insight and guard rails for financial experts and compliance officers, you will learn how to skillfully manage emerging and ongoing cases, understand your fiduciary responsibilities with clarity and build additional guard rails for your enterprise to avoid not only facing fines and bad publicity, but undermining a fulfilling and important career. This is a superb addition to the literature."*—**Dr. Larry Barton, President and CEO, The American College of Financial Services (ret.)**

Introduction

One-Third of a Trillion Dollars

This is a book about compliance and Compliance departments in the world of financial services. Remember to wave your hand in a semicircle with your fingers fanned out while saying "world of finance." It's important because we are talking about everything from the boring bank account or humble credit card to the structured credit default swap or the crypto coin liquidity pool and everything in between. I'll wait. Done? Good.

There's a lot of—self-created—mystery around the workings of finance and yet it's central to every one of our lives. It's like drinking water. We all need it, we all use it, and the powerful political and corporate machinery needed to get it to us is complex, highly lucrative, and therefore an attractive area for greed and corruption. Think *Chinatown* or *Rango*, two movies where the central villain is, essentially, a plumber.

Which is because, paradoxically, finance, like plumbing, is boring. Sooo boring. Put your head down on your desk and roll your eyes at even having to think about banking. Go ahead. It's important. I'll wait. Done? Good.

On the election ballot in Chicago every year, there are three or maybe seven or is it five people on the water reclamation board. I can't remember. I don't feel like Googling it. I really don't. Who cares?

But it is in this combination of boringness and ubiquity that the impact of greed is felt by everyone. There's plenty of room for abuse in water management. Flint, Michigan is one example. Lead pipes in Chicago, most prevalent in poorer areas, are another. Dams in China, Ethiopia, or Colorado cutting off users downstream are others, or the multinational cluster-f that has dried up the Aral Sea. And as I come back to review this chapter, Jackson, Mississippi.

The only way we have discovered as a society to get water turned into something largely boring with limited disasters being the exception is the same way we made anything boring: by collectively forcing the villains to do some good along with the avarice. Water quality standards, highly regulated utilities, licensed plumbers, and so on. That collective action is usually called the law or regulation or Jack Nicholson—the *Chinatown* Jack Nicholson dealing with incest and irrigation, not the *A Few Good Men* "you can't handle the truth" Jack Nicholson. Jack really plays all sides of the ethics here.

This book is my attempt to show something of the inner workings of finance, how regulation has made it appear boring, like water, and yet it hasn't been as consistently safe as a cool glass of H_2O. Put another way, how many national water crisis events have there been in the last 100 years? I mean ones that affect the whole country, not just a city or area? None? Yes, climate change is likely causing the mother of all water crises—and maybe there's some analogy to finance there—but you get my point, most people in the United States have clean, readily available drinking, cooking, and bathing water and most have not lived through a period where that wasn't the case.

In finance, we have a smorgasbord of countrywide (see what I did there?) scale crises in the same time period that affected, directly or indirectly, millions of people: the Great Depression, the Savings and Loan crisis, the dot com collapse, the mortgage crisis, aka, the Global Financial Crisis. And how many scandals? LIBOR, Enron, Worldcom, Countrywide, Lehman Brothers, Bearings, Arthur Anderson, Madoff, and … between 2001 and 2022 there were 561 bank failures in the United States. I'm willing to wager you didn't know. I didn't know until I looked at the Federal Deposit Insurance Corporation (FDIC) website.

Here's another number: ⅓ of a trillion dollars. I kid. It's $339,976,074,213, which is just shy of $4 billion more than ⅓ of a trillion. I thought maybe that you wouldn't notice. What is it? It's the amount of penalties paid by financial institutions between January 2000 and July 2022 when I write this.[1]

---

[1] I picked this cutoff because it was an "even" 12 and a half years. And I had to stop somewhere or I would go mad trying to keep updating all the datasets. I have more recent compliance shenanigan news on my website: www.shcstrategy.com.

A lot of these are multiple hits on the same companies time and time again. Bank of America is currently in the lead at 264, Wells Fargo is working hard to catch up at 222, and JPMorgan and Citigroup are laggards at 199 and 156, respectively. And yet, these are still the largest banks in the country. They are also far from alone, representing, collectively, about 12 percent of the 6,952 individual records identified at violation-tracker.goodjobsfirst.org. If your bank hasn't been fined, you don't have an account at a bank.

At this point, you may be thinking that there's more similarity than difference between Flint water management and predatory subprime mortgage lending, and I would tend to agree with you. All human activity is subject to corruption, greed, ethically questionable activities, predation, and so on. There are pharmaceutical companies making poisonous baby formula, energy companies dumping toxic waste, Takata air bags, Boeing 737 Max, Love Canal, Bhopal, the cumulative total in lives and dollars of humanity's willingness to bend for a buck beggars belief. And no amount of alliteration will make it more palatable.

But I am going to limit myself to finance, because that's what I know most about and I will leave it to you, gentle reader, to generalize to the industry or organization or government of your choice. I am sure you will find parallels.

In every case, there have been put in place a thin line of Compliance and Legal people inside the system trying to keep things on track, but they are, it may seem, given how the failures keep coming, designed to fail. This book is about that curious dichotomy.

Who Is This Book for? And, Who Am I to Write It?

It's for me. I hope it will make me feel better.

It's also for my son, who also hopes I feel better.

But maybe it's also for you. Here are some people I think may enjoy this excursion into the collision zone between corporate governance and the law:

- **Compliance and Legal people**: If you are a compliance or legal department person just starting out and you want to know what it's all about; or you're a jaded and fed-up compliance person and want to shout at a book, *yeah! That's totally right, I knew they were wrong!* And then pump your fist in the air.
- **Regulators**: If you're a regulator and you want to know how to look in the dark heart of banks and bankers.
- **Employee at a financial company**: If you work in a financial company and never understood what Compliance was supposed to be doing.
- **Employee at any kind of company**: If you work in some other industry, Technology, Aerospace, Pharma, and Healthcare, you also never understood what Compliance was supposed to be doing—if you had a Compliance department at all.
- **Student**: If you aspire to get the three letters "MBA" after your name, you should know there's more to a company than spreadsheets.
- **Normal Person**: If you are a normal person and want to know why finance is so full of schemes to take your money— you might like this book.

I have worked at some of the biggest financial firms in the world including Morgan Stanley, JP Morgan Chase, Citigroup, and Wells Fargo. I have worked closely with people from many of the others: Bank of America, UBS, Credit Suisse, Barclays, Royal Bank of Canada, HSBC, PNC, Deutsche Bank, and ones I've either forgotten or who have gone under in one of the many banking crisis events of my generation such as Lehman, Bear Stearns, Countrywide, and so on. I've also worked with regulators and for bosses who were former regulators at most of the institutions discussed earlier.

I have been a customer of nearly every major consulting company's financial and risk and compliance practices and worked closely with senior partners from: McKinsey, KPMG, Ernst & Young, Deloitte, Accenture, Guidehouse, PricewaterhouseCoopers, IBM, and more.

I have been in operational risk, technology risk, compliance, business continuity (aka "disaster recovery" depending if you see the glass half full or the glass smashed to bits on the floor), financial crime, and, at various times, held certifications such as Certified Information Systems Security Professional and Certified Business Continuity Planner—proving that I can answer multiple choice tests and have a company willing to pay several thousand dollars for the privilege. We will cover certification and terms of art such as fiduciary in a later chapter.

That work has been at the intersection of the "C-suite" centers of these big companies and leadership of the regulators in the aftermath of financial crises and the imposition of consent orders,[2] fines, and settlements. I have seen and been an integral part of the responses and the

---

[2] I generally try to avoid footnotes because they make it easier for me as a writer, but annoying for the reader. But when there's a point that really doesn't fit in the flow, I will succumb. And I understand that not everyone knows what a consent order is. Basically, regulators have a variety of "levels" of a...whooping they can dish out. Terminology varies but some commonplace items are MRAs (matters requiring attention), which are private and you have months to fix the problem; MRIAs (matters requiring immediate attention), which are still private but you have only a few weeks to make the fixes—or else; and consent orders, which are the "or else," are public, are posted on the regulators website, and usually have fines and use words like "cease and desist" or "egregious repeated customer harming behavior" in them.

failures and new responses and then new failures as banks try to figure out how to, as one regulator put it, "stop harming customers."

I have been a fly on the wall during the great financial crisis of the turn of the century, and been a cog in the machine attempting to fix the issues with banking that led to that, and many, many previous crises, and I have been a bug ground under the heel of corporate group-think when I realized that we were suffering a collective delusion that the enemy, namely greed mixed with intelligence, could be "fixed" by anyone paid by said enemy.

I have come to this place originally as an outsider. My education was in mathematics and computer science, and my first career was in publishing and helping to transition that industry from print to the web. Back then, I saw a lot of people who didn't grasp what the computer could really do—they tended to think of it as a typewriter on a screen rather than redefining every aspect of publishing—and many others who exploited that confusion to make a quick buck by hoodwinking the first group.

Finance, I have learned, is much the same. Technology supports massive, foundational change on a regular basis, but most people don't understand it in any depth. Jargon, while often useful, provides a smokescreen for the nefarious. With a notable difference. Publishing "innovation" can leave grandma with a box of AOL floppy disks, Encarta CD-ROMs, or a recurring subscription to *Knitting Monthly*. In finance scams, frauds, rug pulls, Ponzi schemes, fiduciary failures, product tying, deceptive acts, identity theft, credit card cloning, "pig butchering" scams, and many more can leave grandma without a house.

CHAPTER 1

A July to Remember

A total of 6,952 violations between 2000 and 2022 is a significant number, and by the time anyone else reads this sentence, there will have been more. Remember, this is also only in the United States. Nevertheless, humans are notoriously innumerate, we are OK with keeping track of three and possibly five or seven items. Here's a picture with 10,000 dots I found with a box I added covering about 6,952.

10,000 dots

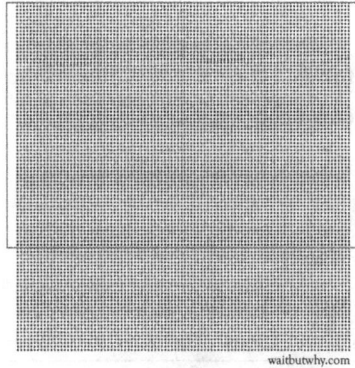

waitbutwhy.com

How about some specific examples? That always helps. I could cherry pick the largest or most egregious or some other curated subset. But what I want to convey is the banality, the pervasiveness, the commonplaceness of financial crime at all levels from small companies to large companies to companies you thought of as dubious to those you, maybe, respected.

And to do that, I'm not going to pick. I'm going to let pure-ish chance select. As I write this it is July 2022. I could have written this chapter in

June or August or any other month or year. It's a bit like throwing a dart blindfolded or letting your financial adviser pick stocks—no, don't do the second one (that's called *foreshadowing*). Also, it is the summer time, and people in finance and government are on vacation, so I may come up empty—no financial crimes this month.

Nope.

The Menagerie of Regulators

To look at the fines, we need to know the players. We will start with the United States and then explore the world. This is because the United States has, for a long time, held a leadership position in terms of financial regulation because of the outsize influence of Wall Street combined with the scale and relative openness of our capital markets. We also have more financial regulators than anyone else. Go USA!

Let's start with a list, and then we will look at each of their activities in July 2022. The list is, I expect, as dull as an airplane butter knife, so I will give you a fun fact for each. Feel free to use them at a cocktail party if you wish to end a conversation.

U.S. Regulators and Hangers on

Regulator	AKA & Estb.	What It Does	"Fun" Facts
U.S. Department of Justice	DOJ Estb. 1870	The long arm of the law	1. No one knows who came up with the official seal, the motto on it, or exactly what it is supposed to mean: *Qui Pro Domina Justitia Sequitur* 2. Can put your a.. in jail
The Office of the Comptroller of the Currency	OCC Estb. 1863	Regulates national banks, that is, banks that operate in multiple states	1. Part of the U.S. Treasury Dept. 2. Established by President Lincoln. Lincoln also created the Secret Service to fight counterfeit currency. Protecting the President came later, unfortunately 3. Concerned with the stability of the financial system 4. Only time you will be expected to spell "comptroller"

Regulator	AKA & Estb.	What it Does	"Fun" Facts
Consumer Financial Protection Bureau	CFPB Estb. 2011	Protect consumers with particular attention on mortgages and unfair and deceptive practices.	1. Created after the 2008 Financial Crisis as part of Dodd–Frank regulation. 2. Took over some rules from the Fed and created their own set of "letter" regulations. 3. Funded by the Fed, but not managed by it. 4. Lots of lawsuits claiming it is unconstitutional. 5. Republicans hate it. They really hate it.
The Securities and Exchange Commission	SEC Estb. 1934	Protect individual investors by regulating public companies.	1. Created in the wake of the 1929 Stock Market Crash. 2. Can ban people from being officers of public companies. 3. Has the EDGAR database of public company filings, where companies compete to comply with filing requirements while still trying to hide executive pay. 4. Has paid over $1 billion to "whistleblowers." 5. Worked with the DOJ to put Martha Stewart in jail.
Financial Industry Regulatory Authority	FINRA Estb. 2007	Stocks and bonds and their brokers and dealers.	1. Not a government organization, but instead an industry self-regulatory body that can levy fines and bar people from the industry. 2. Consolidation of NASD and the member regulation, enforcement and arbitration operations of the New York Stock Exchange, both of which date back to the 1929 Stock Market Crash.
Commodities Futures Trading Commission	CFTC Estb. 1975	Protects the public from abuse in the commodities and futures markets including derivatives, swaps, and other tricksy "financial instruments."	1. In the movie "Trading Places," when Eddie Murphy buys and sells orange juice futures: that's a commodity. 2. Chicago is to commodities as New York is to the stock market. 3. Does it seem like it overlaps with the SEC and FINRA? Pose this question to a crypto conference by asking if NFTs are securities or commodities. Make immediately for the nearest fire exit.

(Continues)

(Continued)

Regulator	AKA & Estb.	What it Does	"Fun" Facts
Office of Foreign Assets Control	OFAC Estb. 1950	Economic sanctions against individuals and countries hostile to the United States.	1. Like the OCC, part of the Treasury. 2. Successor to the Office of Foreign Funds Control (FFC), which had been established during WWII to block money from Nazi Germany. 3. Established as OFAC after China entered the Korean War to freeze all Chinese and North Korean assets.
Board of Governors of the Federal Reserve System	The Fed Estb. 1913	Safety and soundness of the U.S. financial system.	1. The Fed has a national Board of Governors and also 12 regional Federal Reserve System banks. 2. Like the OCC, the Fed is concerned with overall financial system stability. 3. Unlike the OCC, the Fed oversees all banks, including those with state but not national charters. 4. All the big banks are regulated by both the OCC and Fed, which can be confusing for everyone. 5. The Fed loans money to banks at a discount so that the banks can pass on the savings to you (or, as it is, keep the margin for themselves). 6. After the 2008 Financial Crisis many investment banks, such as Morgan Stanley, got remade overnight into regular banks in order to get that "Fed window discount cash" and survive.
Financial Crimes Enforcement Network	FINCEN Estb. 1990	Detect and deter money laundering and other financial abuse.	1. If you take out a bunch of money in cash, FINCEN are the ones who get the "suspicious activity report" (SAR) filing. 2. It's not a perfect system. I got questioned for sending $250 as a Christmas present to a friend who had the same name as a Lieutenant Governor of California. 3. AML/KYC stands for anti-money laundering and know your customer. The government is serious about this because not only are money laundering and fake identities used by criminals—it is a way for said criminals to avoid taxes. And that's the government's money you are messing with now. This is why the largest fines to banks tend to be for failing to prevent money laundering.

Regulator	AKA & Estb.	What it Does	"Fun" Facts
Federal Deposit Insurance Corporation	FDIC Estb. 1933	Protect consumers from bank failures by providing insurance for individual accounts.	1. In the movie "It's A Wonderful Life" Jimmy Stewart doesn't yet have the FDIC and has to beg people not to take all the money out of his bank. 2. Created by the Glass–Steagall Act that also separated investment banks (riskier) from retail banks (safer, except not when the Savings and Loan crisis happened). 3. The 1999 Graham–Leach–Bliley Act erased what was left of Glass–Steagall and was, probably, one of the causes of the 2008 Financial Crisis, which led to the Dodd–Frank Act. Banking law is always there, hyphenated, for the next catastrophe. 4. The FDIC maintains a list of "failed banks." That's always fun when you need a little schadenfreude. 5. The little sticker on teller windows that says "FDIC insured" is regulatory requirement 12 CFR 328.
State Bank Regulators and States' Attorney Generals	No cool AKA Estb. Various	Protect customers of financial firms in their states.	1. New York and California are the most notably active, but other states from Texas to Vermont have been known to go after financial companies in their turf, or to band together with other states for multijurisdictional cage matches. 2. As an example, investment banks are not supposed to do favorable research on companies they also invest in. This was spearheaded by NY's Elliot Spitzer. Depending on your knowledge of Mr. Spitzer the word "spearheaded" was possibly an intentional choice. 3. Each state has their own laws (who knew?) and this includes financial regulation. Owing to the vagaries of, let's call it corruption, some states' laws are copyrighted, meaning you can't legally get them for free. The law is behind a paywall! Admittedly, it's mostly just the sparsely populated state of New Jersey.

(Continues)

(*Continued*)

Regulator	AKA & Estb.	What it Does	"Fun" Facts
Government Sponsored Entities	GSEs Estb. Various	Government-funded entities that are not the government but have government money to hand out for trade, mortgages, student loans, and so on.	They aren't regulators and they don't have regulations, but they do have rules and if you break them you can't have cheap government money—which is, for financial companies, sometimes worse than a fine. They include: • Federal Home Loan Mortgage Corporation (Freddie Mac) • Federal National Mortgage Association (Fannie Mae) • Government National Mortgage Association (Ginne Mae) • SLM Corporation (Sallie Mae) • Export–Import Bank of the United States (ExImBank)
Self-Regulatory Organizations	SROs Estb. Various	Industry groups that provide licensing, training, and have various enforcement means.	They include: • National Futures Association (NFA) • The Financial Planning Association (FPA) • Chicago Board of Trade (CBOT) • American Council of Life Insurers (ACLI) • Fixed Income Clearing Corporation (FICC) • Options Clearing Corporation (also confusingly called the OCC) • American Institute of Certified Public Accounts (AICPA) One form of enforcement for the AICPA is to make you take (shudder) more training.
None of the above	N/A	Bits and pieces of financial management plumbing.	They can fine you for getting your accounting principles wrong and are overseen by the SEC. They include: • Public Company Accounting Oversight Board (PCAOB) • Financial Accounting Standards Board (FASB) Their annual conferences must be just a blast.

Regulators Outside the United States

The rest of the world is often just that: everybody else. These are your D-list celebs who sometimes get the attention, but most often are looking to be in the photo with the Fed. Think the entourage in Entourage. You can pick who you want to be Turtle.

Most other nations suffice themselves with a single regulator or maybe two if they're feeling spicy. Imagine that! Also, most of the regulators are the same as the national bank, like the Fed in the United States. Anyway, here are some of the big ones:

Country	Regulator or Regulators	"Fun" Facts
UK	Financial Conduct Authority, Prudential Regulatory Authority, and Payment Systems Regulator (FCA, PRA and PSR)	The United Kingdom wants to be like the United States, but has only three regulators that are really just suborganizations of one regulator, the Bank of England
EU	European Central Bank and European Banking Authority (ECB and EBA) European Securities and Markets Authority (ESMA)	These folks make regulations that member states implement in their own local laws. So one regulation becomes many. Very fun to figure out all the corner cases
Germany	Bundesanstalt für Finanzdienstleistungsaufsicht (BaFin)	Try saying that after a couple of Jaegermeisters
China	Hong Kong Monetary Authority (HKMA) and China Banking Regulatory Authority (CBIRC)	1. The HKMA used to be one of the most straightforward regulators to deal with 2. This has changed a lot. It's unclear how the regulatory regime will evolve 3. The CBIRC is the opposite. I've heard that working with them requires a bank to send one representative who cannot take any notes in the meeting
Many more	Australia, Mexico, Vietnam, Korea, Singapore, France, Ireland, Switzerland, Sweden, Norway, Finland, Italy, Greece, Israel, UAE, Saudi Arabia, India, Lichtenstein, Isle of Mann, Monaco, Panama, Dominican Republic, Bermuda, Cayman Islands, Native American Tribal Areas, et al.	1. Yes, they all have regulators 2. Switzerland got beat up for allowing a lot of money laundering so their bank accounts aren't as secret as they used to be 3. In general though, the smaller the geographic area, the more you can still hide money there 4. Japan has copies of their regulations in English, but you aren't allowed to rely on them and have to read the Japanese

OK, with all that out of the way, we can see what happened in July.

Time to Run the Numbers: July 2022
Fines and Penalties

U.S. Department of Justice

Note, all text in italics in these sections on penalties are direct cut and paste from the relevant agencies' web pages. Also note, some of these are fines, some are criminal with no fines (but maybe jail time), and some are just the start of the process where the DOJ is filing charges.

July 7   *Addiction Treatment Facilities' Medical Director Sentenced in $112 Million Addiction Treatment Fraud Scheme*

July 8   *Jury Convicts Doctor of Health Care Fraud Scheme*

July 12   *Two Financial Asset Managers Charged in Alleged $1.2 Billion Venezuelan Money Laundering Scheme*

July 13   *Jury Convicts Man of $600 Million Health Care Fraud, Wire Fraud, and ID Theft Scheme*

July 19   *California Man Sentenced to Over 11 Years for $27 Million [Paycheck Protection Program] PPP Fraud Scheme*

July 19   *Three Men Charged in Ecuadorian Bribery and Money Laundering Scheme*

July 20   *Justice Department Charges Dozens for $1.2 Billion in Health Care Fraud*

July 21   *My Big Coin Founder Convicted of Cryptocurrency Fraud Scheme*

July 25   *CEO of Titanium Blockchain Pleads Guilty in $21 Million Cryptocurrency Fraud Scheme*

July 27   *Justice Department and Consumer Financial Protection Bureau Secure Agreement with Trident Mortgage Company to Resolve Lending Discrimination Claims*

Trident is owned by Berkshire Hathaway, which is Warren Buffet's company. More details when we get to the CFPB, including some amazing e-mails. Are you excited to find out?

Also, the medical ones are not fully financial in nature, but they have a large portion of monetary fraud involved, so I think we can keep them in the party.

The Office of the Comptroller of the Currency

Merely one consent order for the OCC, and they had to share with the CFPB. Still better than nothing, though. I've pasted the full text as follows, because I think it's important to be able to see what regulators actually say. However, it's as dry as crackers in my son's backpack.

The too long, didn't read (TL/DR) here is: Bank of America was responsible for unemployment payments to, well, unemployed people. Unemployed folks are notoriously unlikely to buy new cars or invest in stocks and so weren't of value to the bank. Thus, they fell to the bottom of the customer base, got their payments delayed, had their accounts frozen, were the victims of fraudsters stealing their money—you know, poor people stuff.

> July 14
>
> *The Office of the Comptroller of the Currency (OCC) today assessed a $125 million civil money penalty against Bank of America, N.A., for violations of law and unsafe or unsound practices relating to the bank's administration of a prepaid card program to distribute unemployment insurance and other public benefit payments. [...]*
>
> *The OCC's civil money penalty and remediation requirement is separate from, but coordinated with, the Consumer Financial Protection Bureau (CFPB).*

I'm saving the CFPB fine for the next section. Consider it a very short cliff hanger.

Consumer Financial Protection Bureau

July 12   *CFPB Sues ACE Cash Express for Concealing No-Cost Repayment Plans and Improperly Withdrawing Consumers' Funds.* As with the DOJ, this is just a lawsuit being filed, no fines yet.

July 14   *The Bureau issued an order against Bank of America, N.A.* Recall the OCC got $125 million. And the CFPB's penalty was a mere $100 million. I'm sure Bank of America was relieved.

July 26   *Hyundai repeatedly furnished to consumer reporting companies information containing numerous systemic errors and that it knew of many of these inaccuracies for years before attempting to fix them[…] $13,200,000 in redress to affected consumers and a $6,000,000 civil money penalty.*

July 27   *Trident engaged in unlawful discrimination on the basis of race, color, or national origin.* This was joint with the DOJ as noted earlier. The CFPB added on a $4 million fine, more in the following.

July 28   *The Bureau found that U.S. Bank issued credit cards and lines of credit and opened deposit accounts for certain consumers without their knowledge and consent […] U.S. Bank to pay a $37.5 million.*

You may be confusing the U.S. Bank fake accounts with *Consumer Financial Protection Bureau Fines Wells Fargo $100 Million for Widespread Illegal Practice of Secretly Opening Unauthorized Accounts*, but that was a different bank and back in 2016. And that $100 million fine fixed things in the industry, or apparently not.

However, as promised, let's look at Trident, which, as mentioned, is owned by Berkshire Hathaway. This is Warren Buffet, aka the Oracle of Omaha and a paragon of responsible investment and middle-class values.

When I first skimmed the complaint, I saw that it stated, *From 2015 through 2019, Trident operated 53 offices, of which 51 were in majority-white neighborhoods.* And I thought, a business needs to make money and if giving loans where the rich white people lived worked, that's not the most ethical, but also not the most unethical either, is it?

The history here is about "redlining," the practice of not giving mortgages in minority communities that dates back to the 1930s in America. The Federal government sponsored Home Owners' Loan Corporation (HOLC) published maps literally classifying neighborhoods by color and black areas were labeled red meaning hazardous. If you were black you could not get a government-backed mortgage, which meant you couldn't get a mortgage and had to rent. As a knock on, landlords knew this and charged higher rents to minorities as a result.

The Fair Housing Act, Equal Credit Opportunity Act, Fair Lending, and a variety of other regulations attempted to prevent this by requiring regular reporting about fair credit access from mortgage lenders and mandating that they work proactively to make loans.

Trident, for their part, has said, in an e-mail I found quoted on the web: *Trident and any affiliated companies have never denied or discouraged access to mortgage loans or other services based on race. We are committed to continuing to work to find more ways to serve homebuyers in every community we serve.* I was unable to find any statement from Warren Buffet.

Then I read some more of the complaint.

53. In several instances, loan officers or other Trident employees referred to properties in majority-minority areas as being in the "ghetto." For example:

a. A Trident mortgage loan officer e-mailed a Trident online lead coordinator regarding a consumer seeking prequalification, stating: "This one is in the ghetto. pass [sic] it along to ian. HAHA-HAHAHHA kidding."

b. A Trident mortgage loan officer sent an e-mail discussing a comparable property that was used in an appraisal, stating: "This comps [sic] street is like a ghetto and he knows it and if he doesn't that's even worse."

c. A Trident senior loan officer e-mailed another loan officer, stating: "talked to [agent].... He said to stay away from sears street, its [sic] upper ghetto blocked off bad area just a heads up."

54. On another occasion, a Trident assistant loan officer received a racist e-mail entitled "Being White, reminder" from a Fox & Roach employee. The Trident employee forwarded that e-mail to several others. Among other things, the e-mail stated:

a. "Proud to be White;"

b. "You call me 'White boy', 'Cracker', 'Honkey', 'Whitey', 'Caveman' ... And that's OK ... But when I call you Nigger, Kike, Towel head, Sandnigger, Camel Jockey, Beaner, Gook, or Chink ... You call me a racist."

c. "You rob us, carjack us, and shoot at us. But, when a white police officer shoots a black gang member or beats up a black drug dealer running from the law and posing a threat to society, you call him a racist."

d. "There is nothing improper about this e-mail ... But let's see which of you are proud enough to send it on. I sadly don't think many will."

e. "BE PROUD TO BE WHITE!"

55. *On another occasion, a Fox & Roach real estate agent forwarded an e-mail to a Trident loan officer, entitled: "YOU KNOW WHEN YOU'RE IN THE HOOD." The Trident loan officer forwarded the message to several others. The e-mail contained several racist images and racial slurs, including:*

a. A picture of a wheelbarrow filled with watermelons with a sign on the wheelbarrow that said, "Apply for a Credit Card Free Watermelon."

b. A picture purporting to show a liquor store sign with the message "SORRY— CLOSED A NIGGER ROBBED US ... AGAIN."

56. *On another occasion, a Fox & Roach real estate agent forwarded an e-mail to a Trident loan officer and a Trident assistant loan officer with a subject line, "Quick Hide Kit For Illegals." The e-mail contained a video entitled, "Wetback-Quick Hide." The video depicted a man hiding himself in an expandable metal tube.*

Holy @#$!. And it's in the public record, but I'm assuming the details noted previously are not so well known, which is why I cut-and-pasted the parts that show the personal viciousness of financial crimes. People in suits and ties, it seems, can be just as terrible as a cartoon villain. But you knew that, you've been alive for a period of time longer than a day.

Sidebar

E-mail? Really? Are they so dumbass to not know that all electronic communication lives forever? Maybe they were too young on July 25, 2005—July!—to note when:

Wall Street banking giant Morgan Stanley recently suffered an adverse $1.45 billion court judgment, which contributed to a change in leadership at the top. The turning point? The judge's ruling that

Morgan Stanley had acted in "bad faith" in failing to turn over relevant e-mails. "The storage folks found an additional 1,600 backup tapes in a closet," explained a Morgan Stanley executive.

But have they not been drunk and woken up the next day and looked at their sent messages? So maybe don't use e-mail to say terrible things. And don't use some nonwork messaging platform either:

December 2021, JPMorgan Admits to Widespread Recordkeeping Failures and Agrees to Pay $125 Million Penalty to Resolve SEC Charges. Firm also agrees to implement significant improvements to its compliance controls[…]

As described in the SEC's order, JPMS admitted that from at least January 2018 through November 2020, its employees often communicated about securities business matters on their personal devices, using text messages, WhatsApp, and personal e-mail accounts.

Compliance controls got a shout out. That's nifty.

The Securities and Exchange Commission

The SEC is maybe who you think of first when you think of a financial regulator. They're the ones who put Martha Stewart in jail. This month they had the following:

July 18   *[C]harges against Equitable Financial Life Insurance Company for providing account statements to about 1.4 million variable annuity investors that included materially misleading statements and omissions concerning investor fees. Equitable agreed to pay $50 million to harmed investors, most of whom are public school teachers and staff members.*

July 20   *[C]harges against Health Insurance Innovations (HII) and its former CEO Gavin Southwell for concealing extensive consumer complaints about short-term and limited health insurance products HII offered.*

July 21   *Charges Former Coinbase Manager, Two Others in Crypto Asset Insider Trading Action*

July 25   *[A]lleges insider trading by investment banker Brijesh Goel and his friend Akshay Niranjan, who was a foreign exchange trader at a large financial institution.*

July 25   *[A]lleges that Seth Markin, a former FBI trainee, and his friend Brandon Wong made approximately $82,000 and $1.3 million, respectively, from illegally trading ahead of the February 2021 announcement of a tender offer by Merck & Co., Inc., to acquire Pandion Therapeutics, Inc.*

July 25   *Charges Former Indiana Congressman with Insider Trading. Stephen Buyer allegedly used inside information to buy $1.5 million in stocks.*[1]

July 27   *SEC Charges JPMorgan, UBS, and TradeStation for Deficiencies Relating to the Prevention of Customer Identity Theft.* Fines as follows: *JPMorgan: $1.2 million, UBS: $925,000, and TradeStation: $425,000.*

The SEC also launched complaints against a bunch of individuals listed as follows. None of these are officially decided yet, and therefore not in the total count of 6,952 violations above. Also, individual sanctions are also not part of the total. Further, I have no idea how many thousands of them are there, but extrapolating from this one random month (plus FINRA ones as follows), maybe 1,000 a year or 20,000+ since the year 2000?

That's this many:

10,000 dots

10,000 dots

---

[1] Not much will come of this. Later in the book I'll talk about the lack of dentition for the SEC when it comes to members of Congress.

July 1	*Justin R. Kimbrough,*	July 15	*John David McAfee and*
	Terry Nikopoulos. TKJ		*Jimmy Gale Watson, Jr.*
	Investments Corp.,	July 15	*Richard Jonathan Eden,*
	TKJ Holdings Corp.,		*et al.*
	Preeminent Trade Group	July 18	*Bruce Schoengood,*
	Inc., The Elyte Group		*Medifirst Solutions, Inc.,*
	Corp., and Prosperity		*and Joshua Tyrell*
	Consultants, LLC	July 21	*Apostolos Trovias*
July 1	*Eric S. Hollifield*	July 25	*Brijesh Goel and Akshay*
July 1	*Matthew Wade Beasley,*		*Niranjan**
	et al.	July 25	*Stephen E. Buyer, et al.**
July 1	*William Glen Baker,*	July 26	*Todd Lahr and Thomas*
	Michael Bowen, Cannon		*Megas*
	Operating Company LLC,	July 26	*Seth Markin and Brandon*
	North Texas Minerals		*Wong*
	LLC, and Chol Kim	July 26	*Amit Bhardwaj, et al.**
	(a/k/a Brandon Kim)	July 27	*Alexandra Robert,*
July 6	*Sung Mo Jun, Joon Jun,*		*Chalala Academy LLC*
	Junwoo Chon, Ayden Lee,	July 27	*Frank Okunak*
	and Jae Hyeon Bae	July 28	*Mark Klein, et al.*
July 6	*Carrillo et al.;*	July 28	*GP Capital Group,*
July 7	*George W. Haywood*		*Inc. and Shannon W.*
July 7	*Doron A. Tavlin, Afshin*		*Illingworth*
	Farahan, and David J.	July 28	*Patient Access Solutions,*
	Gantman		*Inc., et al.*
July 11	*Jerry Li*	July 28	*Robert L. Murray, Jr.*
July 11	*Shimon Rosenfeld*	July 29	*Alan Z. Appelbaum*
July 13	*Manuel Alvis, Joseph*		
	Boulos, Carlos Pingarron,		
	Carlos Sorondo		

A * indicates duplicates from the initial list of SEC items at the start of this section.

What do these complaints allege? Here are some excerpts from the last one to give you a flavor. Poor Alan Applebaum, cursed with a last and first name to always bring him to the top of the list.

UNITED STATES DISTRICT COURT SOUTHERN DISTRICT OF FLORIDA U.S. SECURITIES AND EXCHANGE COMMISSION, Plaintiff, v. ALAN Z. APPELBAUM, Defendant.

[... boring intro stuff omitted ... Google if you so desire, it's a public record!...]

from July 2017 to May 2019, Appelbaum made over 140 unsuitable recommendations and purchases of highly complex structured products for seven retail customers. [...] Appelbaum knew, was reckless in not knowing, or should have known that these securities were unsuitable for those customers. [...]

Appelbaum omitted the material fact that his customers could lose some or all of their principal investment. [...] Appelbaum also executed hundreds of unauthorized trades in the same seven customers' brokerage accounts without their consent [...] Appelbaum received compensation for the vast majority of the unauthorized and unsuitable trades [...] Appelbaum received at least $1 million in compensation.

Some of Appelbaum's customers, by contrast, suffered significant losses, including one customer who lost over $1 million and another who lost over $200,000 [...]

The rest of the violations are much the same: financial industry "professionals" using some combination of complex terminology, misleading or incomplete information, and trusting customers to profit unscrupulously.

Financial Industry Regulatory Authority

FINRA action in July, namely sanctions against companies.

July 15   *Bank of America Securities* published 107 inaccurate monthly reports of order executions, and received a censure (a trifecta!) and a $325,000 fine.

July 18   *Wilson-Davis & Co., Inc.* got a censure and a $100,000 fine for *deficiencies in the reserves in its special reserve bank account for the exclusive benefit of customers.*

July 20   *Sagetrader, LLC* got a censure and a $775,000 fine for failure to *reasonably supervise for potentially manipulative trading on its platforms.*

FINRA, like the SEC, also goes after individuals. The term of art is Letters of Acceptance, Waiver, and Consent (AWC), which are simply that, nastygrams saying you broke a rule, and if you accept our judgment, which is usually a fine and being barred from the industry for some period of time, we won't come after you beyond that. Nice, right? Here's the AWCs sent to individuals for July 2022:

July 6	Wei Donald Tang	July 19	James Daniel Kent
July 7	David Karandos	July 19	Michael Hong Cho
July 7	William Edward Torriente	July 20	David Hixon*
July 7	Charles Scott Burford**	July 21	Adam Thomas Marquardt
July 11	Michael Ohlemacher	July 25	Gregory Scott Hanshew*
July 12	Stephen G. Whitman*	July 26	Brian Harold Young
July 13	Franz H. Lambert	July 26	Richard A. Hogan
July 13	Brandon Autiero	July 27	Stephen R. Green
July 13	Harris Kausar	July 27	Lance E. Baraker
July 14	Daniel L. Bicket	July 27	Robert W. Vial
July 15	David G. Menashe	July 28	Wayne von Borstel
July 15	Robin Lee Taliaferro	July 28	Joseph A. Ambrosole
July 19	Francis Joseph Velten*		

Those with an * technically didn't get an AWC letter because they were unable to be found as FINRA documents at length via many attempts at *[respondents] last known residential address*. Which prevented, in one case, *investigation into whether Hixon improperly borrowed from a customer, whether Hixon repaid that customer, and whether and why Hixon solicited other customers and co-workers for loans*.

The lone ** entry is a case where a financial adviser chose to argue that he had not done wrong and showed up at FINRA to do just that. For his troubles, he was fined $10,000 and barred for six months.

Picking another example, this time chronologically, we'll take the last one in July, Mr. Wayne von Borstel.

[…] instead of identifying the young beneficiaries on the account forms, he identified adults who were related to the young beneficiaries, typically a parent, as each account's beneficiary. By doing so, Von Borstel enabled these new accounts to bypass [his employer's] review under its new 529 plan policy and caused [his employer's] books and records to be inaccurate.

It looks like Wayne didn't want the overhead of paperwork, or, maybe, he thought that the accounts wouldn't get opened if he did fill it in correctly and he didn't want to anger his customers and potentially lose them. Instead, he got a 15-day suspension from the industry and a $5,000 fine.

You may read the rest at your leisure on the FINRA website.

Commodity Futures Trading Commission

Almost $50 million this month for the CFTC. Not bad, but we missed, by just one day, on June 30, a $1.7 billion fraud involving Bitcoin. But that's the distant past in finance, so never mind.

July 5 *J.P. Morgan to Pay $850,000 for Swap Reporting Failures.*

July 5 *Swap Dealer [BNP Paribas] to Pay $6 Million for Swap Reporting and Daily Mark Disclosure Violations.*

July 7 *Federal Court Orders Texas Unregistered Commodity Pool Operator [David Seibert, et al.] to Pay More Than $13 Million[2] for Commodity Fraud.*

July 15 *Over $29 Million [on Financial Tree, et al.] in Restitution and Penalties Against California and Colorado Residents.*

July 18 *Texas Man [Jimmy Gale Watson, et al.] to Pay Over $290,000 for Manipulative and Deceptive Digital Asset Pump-and-Dump Scheme [See also SEC individuals].*

July 19 *Powerline Petroleum, LLC to Pay $875,000 For Fraud, False Statements to CME, and Failure to Register as a Commodity Trading Advisor.*

---

[2] $13,073,361

Office of Foreign Assets Control

Only two for OFAC.

> July 12 Amex agreed to remit $430,500 to settle its potential civil liability for 214 apparent violations of OFAC's Kingpin sanctions. (Extra points for the cool name "Kingpin sanctions."
>
> July 21 MidFirst Bank (MidFirst) for violations of the Weapons of Mass Destruction Proliferators Sanctions Regulations (WMDPSR). (Yikes!)

Board of Governors of the Federal Reserve System aka the Fed

Just one minnow. Not a great month for the Fed. Back in February there was the *Federal Reserve Board announces $20.4 million penalty against the National Bank of Pakistan, a foreign bank operating in the United States and headquartered in Pakistan, for anti-money laundering violations.* But that's even further back than June. That's practically last year.

> July 7 Easthampton Savings Bank had *a pattern or practice of violations under Section 102(f)(2) of the [Flood Insurance] Act, 42 U.S.C. § 4012a(f)(2)* and is fined $17,000, which the bank pays, but admits no wrongdoing. This seems to be a first for Easthampton, so well done there? Although it is owned by Hometown Financial who has a couple of other puny fines amounting to less than $100,000.

Financial Crimes Enforcement Network

None. Nada. Zippo. If this had been March, we would have seen the company USAA get a penalty of $140,000,000 minus $60,000,000 money penalty imposed by the OCC for "pervasive" and "repeated" failures in allowing money laundering. But it's July, so all's well!

Federal Deposit Insurance Corporation

Lest you think the FDIC always swings low, they have made some big hits. For example, Banamex (Citigroup's Mexico subsidiary) was fined $140,000,000 for money laundering by the FDIC in July 2015. But not so much this July:

July 1   Mount Vernon Bank and Trust Company. Failed to provide information about flood insurance. Penalty: $2,500 fine.

July 12   Blue Hills Bank, Rushell T. Harris. Bank teller used customers' identities to open fake accounts. Penalty: can't work at banks anymore.

July 12   Investors Bank, Tiffany Zemlachenko. Bank teller embezzled $42,000. Penalty: can't work at banks anymore.

July 13   Security State Bank. Also flood insurance missteps. Penalty: $6,000 fine.

July 28   Lincoln 1st Bank. On July 28, the FDIC lifted a consent order against Lincoln 1st Bank because they were being acquired by Ion bank.

The Lincoln 1st Bank (or Lincoln Bancorp) item is a puzzler. A consent order was made against them in January 2022 and was one of the most severe I've ever seen. It required the board of directors to make new policies, prove that they were meeting, and make all kinds of reports about how the bank was going to remain solvent. However, I can't find a single news article or other about this bank or what the hell it did to piss off the FDIC so much. But here we are in July, and poof, consent order lifted. Weird.

Around the World

Here's some quotes from regulators across the globe:

July 15   *FCA [UK] fines The TJM Partnership Limited (in liquidation) £2 million for serious financial crime control failings in relation to cum-ex trading*

July 4   *BaFin [Germany] imposed administrative fines totalling 11,290,000 euros on Steinhoff International Holdings N.V.*

July 20   *The Securities and Futures Commission (SFC) [Hong Kong] has reprimanded RBC Investment Services (Asia) Limited (RBC) and fined it $7.7 million for regulatory breaches relating to mishandling of client assets.*

At this point, I am stopping and not just because there's only so many regulatory websites in English.

Wrapping Up July 2022

US DOJ	$20,000,000 and also jail time. Years and years of jail.
SEC	$52,550,000
FINRA	$1,200,000 with the small individual fines omitted
OCC	$125,000,000
CFPB	$160,700,000
CFTC	$49,300,861
Treasury	$430,500
Fed	$17,000
FINCEN	$0 😵
FDIC	$50,500
FCA	£2,000,000 or $2,456,810.00 USD at August 1 rate
BaFin	€11,290,000 or $11,576,314.40 USD
SFC	$7,700,000 HKD or $980,896.84 USD
Total	**$423,281,985.40**

That's no August 2014 when it was announced *Bank of America to Pay $16.65 Billion in Historic Justice Department Settlement for Financial Fraud Leading up to and During the Financial Crisis*, but the year is only half over.

I suppose it should go without saying, but these are the indictments and penalties that were made. I have, by necessity, not included those people and companies who have, at least for now, not been discovered. Do the regulators get the majority of criminal activity or is it a metaphorical iceberg with grift, small and large, largely unseen? I don't know, but I have my suspicions, and you probably do too after seeing what one unassuming month looks like.

Moving on.

CHAPTER 2

What Is Compliance?

The Oldest Profession

The need for compliance isn't just for grandma and you and erroneous charges on some poor soul's Diners Club Card—I was going to make some snide comment about Diners Club and that you are probably surprised it still exists, if you had even ever heard of it, but look, it does, and it gives you access to some not-where-you-will-ever-be airport lounges. And I learned that one of those lounges is the @9tysix Lounge in Abuja Nnamdi Azikiwe Intl (ABV), Nigeria, with the following picture on the Diners Club website.

I'm speaking from a nonexpert position here, but if you are a VIP, do you want to be sitting behind a giant red-with-drop-shadow-three-foot-tall "VIP" sign set in a larger, transparent window? Is this where Elon

Musk hangs out? Who am I kidding, I'm sure he does. I think I see his feet on the right.

Anyhow, July 2022 is not, as I said, an exception. Compliance issues are as old as human society. In 1750 BCE, or so, a person named Nanni wrote a complaint to his copper dealer, Ea-nasir, in the city of Ur. The clay tablet of this missive now sits in the British Museum. The copper wasn't up to snuff. It wasn't quality assured or quality controlled in Nanni's view. We have no idea what Ea-nasir responded nor if Nanni subsequently took matters up with the Babylonian Commodities Exchange. Nevertheless, a customer complaint about a commodity is certainly a Compliance issue.

Let's take something more modern, but older than the abovementioned Diners Club. The namesake of my alma mater is one Daniel Drew. He was a robber baron, a train tycoon, and an all-round misbegotten jerk, as best I can figure. He, and his even more dubious friends, Jay Gould and James Fisk, competed with Vanderbilt.

Vanderbilt had bought up all of the rights for rail that went north from Manhattan. Side note: this is why, to this day, a train to Boston from Penn Station heads East to Long Island, makes a big loop West to the Bronx, and then back East to Boston. The shorter route North was owned by Vanderbilt so they had to route around him!

Drew had already created the concept of watered stock earlier in his career. And by stock and water, I mean cattle and water. Daniel drove cattle from upstate to the Bulls Head market in lower Manhattan and didn't let them have water or food for over a day. He'd stop in what is now Central Park and let the cattle drink their fill—and they were thirsty—thus adding weight to the cows and money to his pocket. Innovation!

Later Drew got into railroads and he repeated his trick. He was working with the Erie railroad and trying to keep Vanderbilt from buying it. So he used a similar concept to adding water to stock. And by stock and water, I mean stock and more stock. As Vanderbilt attempted to buy a majority, Drew just printed more stock. Vanderbilt, being ludicrously wealthy, kept buying. This was not terrible for Drew, as he got paid for all the stock he printed.

Ultimately, Vanderbilt wrested control and then attempted to get all of that extra stock Drew printed deemed illegal. The two sides took their fight to the NY legislature in Albany, where each of them set up shop on different floors of the same tavern—across the street from said legislature. The senators happened by, as it happens, and were bribed on one floor, went upstairs, were bribed some more, and then went back down to see if they could do it again. There was an unusual amount of cardio for the senators that day.

To repeat: Vanderbilt was ludicrously wealthy, and so he won. Drew, Gould, and Fisk's stock printing was declared illegal, and so the three fled from the long arm of the NY law. Which meant, at the time, New Jersey. By dark of night, with a canoe, oars, and lots of stock (the paper kind), they rowed to NJ and set up a fort in, what else, a tavern. Armed guards and all. Ultimately, all was settled, no one was shot, and Drew lived to do more wheeling and dealing, amassing a great fortune, and then squandering it, and pissing off people all along the way. He died penniless, but his former mansion in Madison, New Jersey, was bequeathed via a Methodist school as a way of hopefully getting him somewhere better in the afterlife. This is why the Methodist archives of America are at Drew University—which is something you almost certainly didn't think was useful to know.

What's the point? The point is that financial crime is in the eye of the beholder, and that beholder is usually the aggrieved party. And if the beholder is rich and powerful, it's probably a crime. And if not, it's probably a payday loan.

Let us move on then to a question that like art and obscenity has no answer beyond, "I know it when I see it."—namely, what is compliance?

What Is Compliance?

On the face of it, compliance is a straightforward concept. Comply with the law. Stop at stop signs and don't murder. Easy peasy. Lemon. Squeezy. That's what is referred to as lowercase "c" compliance. Capital "C" compliance is the department that works to enable everybody else in the company to comply.

I intentionally said "works to enable." You may have expected "ensures." I myself wrote that word and then deleted it and wrote "makes sure" and then deleted that. I tried "improves" but that got the backspace also. This is ingrained behavior from years of PowerPoint slides where such wording was routinely scrubbed.

This is because nobody at a bank wants to promise to ensure anything. On one hand, it's—and I would say rightly—viewed that the ultimate responsibility to comply with the law lies with the frontline business units that deal with customers. This is as opposed to Compliance, which along with Technology, Finance, and so on are "second-line of defense." The third line is Audit, by the way, giving this approach the duly named "three lines of defense model." As another note, nobody agrees where Legal falls into this mix.

Hold on, Compliance isn't Legal? I was just getting my mind around the fact that Compliance doesn't ensure compliance—and I wasn't sure I agreed. Surely Legal is part of Compliance? No. Nope. Nada. And this is partly because Legal, and lawyers, are viewed in banks as, I struggle for the right word, "refined?" I was also thinking "superior." And I'm married to a lawyer who is also a Compliance officer.

Again, hold on. Not all Compliance officers are lawyers? Again no. In some banks Legal and Compliance are one function. In those cases, Legal and the general counsel (GC) is invariably the senior to the junior chief compliance officer (CCO).

In other banks, Legal and Compliance are separate, often by preference of the regulators. After the mortgage crisis, several consent orders, which are the official and public shaming of a financial firm by a regulatory agency, forced the split between Legal and Compliance. They also required that the CCO role has "stature" in the organization and not be subordinate to a business unit head.

A cynic might say that Legal's job is to defend the bank and will potentially argue that turning off grandma's electricity was perfectly legal and in case of fire start up the shredders, whereas Compliance's job is to hand over the documents before they can be turned into confetti.

Citigroup is a notable example where Legal and Compliance were forced to unite. The reason for the change of course at Citigroup is between them and their regulator, but I suspect it's because after years of failure to cure compliance failings the regulator took the approach we all take with the old USB ports. Just try turning it over and shoving it in again.

At the banks where Compliance is not part of Legal, it is usually part of Risk. What is Risk? Risk has three primary categories and lots of subcategories. It is both as exciting as it sounds and something nearly every bank redoes every other year in a cycle of hoping that maybe if we label things differently it won't look so bad when we show the regulators—although again, that would be cynical of me to say. (In reality, risk taxonomy editing is a program for consultants to keep them employed.)

The three risk categories, like animal, vegetable, and mineral, are as follows:

1. Market risk
2. Credit risk
3. Operational risk

Market risk is the risk that the market goes against you. That is, your bank is heavily invested in tech stocks and tech stocks tank and you run out of money. Liquidity risk is a related concept where you maybe have enough assets, but they are "illiquid," meaning they can't be sold quickly, like houses or paintings of dogs playing card games. The mortgage crisis of 2007 was essentially a market risk event.

Credit risk is the risk of any individual counterparty not paying up. The evaluation of credit risk is the domain of underwriting departments who attempt to figure out how likely it is you can and will pay your debts on time. This ranges from consumers and their credit scores to countries and their ratings.

Operational risk is literally everything else that can go wrong. The computer blows up. The building catches fire. The fire department douses everything with water, turning all the paper files to mush. The cleaning company hired to get rid of the mess steals credit card numbers they reconstruct by salvaging the wet paper and hanging it to dry in a secret lab in Belarus.

Or the problem could be coming from outside the house. Customers could be laundering drug money through the bank. This has an element of credit risk and maybe even market risk. So maybe you want to reclassify? It's very easy to keep talking about where we think the sofa should go, and then moving it a little left, a little right, and never getting on with the hard work of sitting on the sofa.

Some of the types of operational risk are the following:

- Business continuity—aka disaster recovery, but that's negative sounding. When presenting to management, there are no bad things, only opportunity. For example, a hole in the road your car tire broke off in isn't a "pothole," it's a "vehicular maintenance improvement opportunity."
- Information security—this means keeping information secure. As names go, it's one of the better ones.
- Privacy—this is broad, it means customer and employee "personally identifiable information" (PII) must be protected. PII is pronounced pee-eye-eye. Not pi-i-i which it looks like.
- Collusion—this is basically impossible to stop in any simple way. When two or more people are working to subvert the system, someone else is required to discover the activity. It's so hard to stop that one of the most common controls is consecutive leave. That is, everyone in a job where they might collude to steal money has to take their vacation in a solid block, usually two weeks minimum. The idea is that sometime during that two weeks a package shows up on the vacationing person's desk and someone filling in says, "hey, what's this brown paper wrapped stack of $100 bills?" Really.
- Market manipulation—for example, trying to corner the market and doing a "pump and dump." This is common in thinly traded and poorly regulated markets, think cryptocurrency and penny stocks, but people still try it all the time in larger markets. Tech stocks, copper, onions.[1] You know, all the regular stuff.

---

[1] Given the vagaries of web links breaking over time, I'm not going to be linking to every scheme and law breaking. It's the modern world, if you want to know more about Bill Hwang, Siegel, and Kosuga, or Yasuo Hamanaka, you know where Google is.

- Insider trading—this is the one where your cousin knows the CFO of that big company and that they are buying that other big company and you buy the stock—and then you go to jail. Maybe your name is Martha Stewart.
- Money laundering—this was explained best in the TV show *Breaking Bad* both directly by Saul Goodman in a nail salon and in operation through the carwash where Sklyer rings up fake receipts.
- "Fat finger" errors—where someone types $10,000 instead of $1,000. I don't like the blame being placed on finger mass, and I didn't come up with the name, but "typo" sounds too minor for what can easily be an order of magnitude problem.
- "I'm sure" errors. This one I did just name, right here, right now. It doesn't have a name, but it happens all the time. This is when someone overrides the alarm bells or warning messages and clicks "yes, I meant to do that" when they really didn't.
- Scheduled system maintenance (what if it doesn't turn back on?)
- Programming errors—there are three kinds of programming errors: name, conflicts, and off-by-one errors. That's my programming joke I learned in college and I'm proud to reuse it here.
- Incorrect policies or procedures—but it didn't say "A dog *can't* play basketball."
- Misleading or omitted disclosures or reporting—we didn't tell you that we bet against the deal we sold you? Our name is Goldman Sachs and you are a savvy customer and so we didn't need to. Stopping looking at us.
- Failure to know your customer (KYC)—we received a lot of money in your account in ones and fives in our branches around the country and you withdrew $100 bills in towns on the Mexico border. Nothing to see here, right?
- Discrimination of customers based on ethnicity, race, sexual orientation, and so on—"we'd be happy to talk to your husband..." This actually happened to my wife. Luckily, not at a bank, but at a resort where they were trying to sell us a

timeshare. That was not a big deal. Actual discrimination is a real problem both in the past, see "redlining," and still today, see "payday loans," "minimum account balances," and so on.

- Unfair or deceptive acts—this is everything from fine print saying that after the introductory period the interest rate goes to 2,000 percent to advertising mortgages in Spanish, opening accounts in Spanish, then sending default and foreclosure notices in English. Which, of course, happened.

These are, as noted earlier, not exactly mutually exclusive or comprehensively exhaustive (MECE), meaning that there will be, as mentioned, lots of opportunity to rebucket everything time and time again. Also, the acronym "MECE" is pronounced "mee cee" and is great to toss out in the taxonomy refresh session where people are focused on their own peccadillos rather than, say, figuring out how to stop bad behavior. Having said "MECE" at such meetings myself, I can confirm no one will be impressed, but they will mark you for future reference as a smartass-slash-potential troublemaker.

Let's now connect the risks stated earlier with the law and compliance: one way things can go sideways is if they are done in a manner that violates the law or causes a lawsuit. This is true of all operational risks. If things can go wrong, such as ATMs going down due to a power outage, there would have been lawsuits, and subsequently, regulations—see Regulation CC that mandates the availability of depositors' funds.

In a related sense, if it can go wrong, then going wrong can potentially be used as part of an illegal activity. That was a confusing sentence. What I mean is, the ATMs going down could just be because of a lightning storm. Or, it could be because the bank is about to go under and wants to pay out the board of directors first and slowing down the depositors might make that easier. Again, see cryptocurrency, but also anytime historically when there have been limits imposed on withdrawals. The reasons may be technical or not or a bit of both.

Compliance is the department responsible for putting in place systems and controls to reduce the risk of breaking the law within the operational processes of a company.

Great. Good. And, you will not be surprised, not wholly correct. Here's an example, who's responsible for privacy? There are multiple aspects here. Of course, there are regulations: U.S. banking Regulation P, the EU's Global Data Protection Act (GDPR), California Consumer Privacy Act (CCPA), and privacy aspects of regulations across the board of consumer protection, investment banking, and human resources. However, the implementation of the policies, processes, and computer systems will be done by the Technology department.

So who is in charge of reducing the privacy risk? Where will the experts reside? Compliance maybe? Technology probably. Because privacy isn't just knowing the rules, it's figuring out how to build systems and processes to manage both the rules and the organization's privacy framework. That is, maybe the rules say you have to protect customers' personally identifiable information, and to do that, industry best practice is to encrypt all production data.

Because there's an overlap between business goals and regulations, and there is, by necessity, a decision made by management about *how* to and *how much* to control for risk, based on management's view of the risk, the expertise is usually required both in Compliance and in Technology, or HR, or Finance, or the business itself. For example, if you are a company with millions of customers, privacy is one kind of thing, but if you are a family office with literally one customer, it's something else. This is an eternal conundrum for Compliance departments. What is in Compliance and what is in some other back office function's domain or even in the front line? It's not straightforward.

I have worked in Compliance where Compliance was part of Legal or part of Risk or part of Operational Risk. I have worked in Technology Risk, which was part of Technology, and not Risk or Compliance. I have worked in Operational Risk and have been at odds with the Compliance department. I have worked in Oversight and Control—can you get more Orwellian sounding?—where I was part of the chief operating officer function and was at odds with separate Compliance and Legal departments.

So while everyone can agree we must comply with the law, in the final analysis, no one can agree where Compliance belongs in the organization: Legal, Risk, Technology, HR, Finance, or the "frontline" business itself. And this is one of the reasons compliance, lowercase, is hard to achieve.

Oh, and no one agrees on the law.

What Is the Law?

I have had some interesting conversations in my time in finance. Here are a few examples:

> "The list of laws that we have to comply with. Do you have that in a spreadsheet or something?"—asked of a CCO.
>
> "Don't ask that."—response from the CCO.
>
> "What does this law require?"—asked of a GC.
>
> "It depends. Are we suing someone over this or is someone suing us?" —response from the GC.
>
> "Is this legal?"—asked of lots of lawyers and Compliance officers, many times.
>
> "The current environment and industry approach to this is that it is [high, moderate, low] risk to participate in the activity described in the manner considered as presented to me on this day and time and…."

Or, to put it another way, you keep using that word the "law," I don't think it means what you think it means.

Let me take an example, Regulation Z, aka Truth in Lending Act, aka TILA, says, in section 1026.19 part a, subpart 1, paragraph i:

> **Time of disclosures.** *In a reverse mortgage transaction subject to both § 1026.33 and the Real Estate Settlement Procedures Act (12 U.S.C. 2601 et seq.)* that is secured by the consumer's dwelling, the creditor shall provide the consumer with good faith estimates of the disclosures required by § 1026.18 and shall deliver or place them in the mail not later than **the third business day** after the creditor receives the consumer's written application.

I highlighted the part about "the third business day." Well that's easy, right? Three days. Today is Tuesday, I just got your application, I have to get an estimate of the disclosures (as described in Section 1026.18) to you by, checks fingers, Friday. If I send it to you on Friday, I'm in violation of the law. Slap the fine on me.

But Friday is Good Friday this week. My bank was founded on Christian principles and we never work on holy days. And Saturday and Sunday clearly aren't business days. So I have until Monday. Done.

Hang on, your branches are open on Saturdays. You do business on Saturday. You missed the date. I'm telling the regulators on you. Although they are closed today, I swear I'll tell them.

Not so fast. You are talking about Saturday May 4, 2019, aka Greenery Day, aka Japanese Arbor day, and that is a holiday. Did we mention that we are a Christian and Shinto principled business? We strictly follow all related holidays.

Rinse, litigate, repeat.

This is why the CFPB helpfully provides "official commentary" on the regs to try to explain things like "business day." To wit:

> **Timing and use of estimates.** *The disclosures required by § 1026.19(a)(1)(i) must be delivered or mailed not later than three business days after the creditor receives the consumer's written application. The general definition of "business day" in § 1026.2(a)(6)—a day on which the creditor's offices are open to the public for substantially all of its business functions—is used for purposes of § 1026.19(a)(1)(i). See comment 2(a)(6)-1.* **This general definition is consistent with the definition of "business day" in Regulation X—a day on which the creditor's offices are open to the public for carrying on substantially all of its business functions.** *See 12 CFR 1024.2. Accordingly, the three-business-day period in § 1026.19(a)(1)(i) for making early disclosures coincides with the time period within which creditors subject to RESPA must provide good faith estimates of settlement costs. If the creditor does not know the precise credit terms, the creditor must base the disclosures on the best information reasonably available and indicate that the disclosures are estimates under § 1026.17(c)(2). If many of the disclosures are estimates, the creditor may include a statement to that effect (such as "all numerical disclosures except the late-payment disclosure are estimates") instead of separately labeling each estimate. In the alternative, the creditor may label as an estimate only the items primarily affected by unknown information. (See the commentary*

to § 1026.17(c)(2).) The creditor may provide explanatory material concerning the estimates and the contingencies that may affect the actual terms, in accordance with the commentary to § 1026.17(a)(1).

As you can see, it's covered in Regulation X, where it says, "a day on which…" And you can see where there's still plenty of room to argue. *Yes, we were open on Saturday, but only for people to put staples in their passbooks, not for "substantially all" of our business functions.*

Of course, that's just Regulation X. Here's a little table of what a business day can mean.

CFPB Regulation	Business Day Is
Regs E and X	Any day on which the financial institution's offices are open to the public for carrying on substantially all business functions
Reg C and DD	Any day other than Saturday, Sunday, or any legal public holiday
Reg Z	Mostly the same as E and X, except, for the below where it's the same as C and DD • Rescission. The imposition of fees in connection with a reverse mortgage • The waiting period after providing reverse mortgage disclosures • The seven-business-day waiting period following the provision of the loan estimate • The mail delivery of a loan estimate, closing disclosure, or private education loan disclosures • The fee restriction before the intent to proceed • The provision of revised loan estimates • The provision of the closing disclosure • The provision of the escrow account cancelation notice, high-cost mortgage disclosures, and reverse mortgage disclosures
CFPB Reg CC	Same as C and DD, except *banking day* is also defined. Meaning it can be a business day, but not a banking day
CFPB Reg B, O, P, V	No official guidance

This is just the CFPB, one U.S. regulator. For example, the Bank Secrecy Act defines: *A day, as normally communicated to its depository customers, on which a bank routinely posts a particular transaction to its customer's account.* It's a mess. In the case, *Mayoral v. WMC Mortgage LLC et al.*, the judge got all tied in knots about what a business day is:

> *The real debate is whether the Monday following Christmas should constitute a business day. The regulations provide that, for purposes of rescission, the term business day "means all calendar days except Sundays and the legal public holidays specified in 5 U.S.C. 6103(a), such as New Year's Day, the Birthday of Martin Luther King, Jr., Washington's Birthday, Memorial Day, Independence Day, Labor Day, Columbus Day, Veterans Day, Thanksgiving Day, and Christmas Day."12 C.F.R. § 226.2(a)(b). Accordingly, Saturdays are business days, but holidays are not business days for purposes of rescission. Sometimes, a holiday falls on a Saturday or a Sunday, and, in that event, the legal holiday is usually the preceding Friday or the following Monday. In 2005, for example, the legal holiday of Christmas was observed on Monday, December 26, 2005. How does one calculate business days when a holiday falls on a Saturday or a Sunday?*

And it goes on like this for a couple more pages.

Did you know there was a lawsuit decided on a single comma? And that there have been many lawsuits over words and the interpretation of those words and that some of these cases have dragged on for years and gone back and forth for plaintiff or defendant in that time and all the way to the Supreme Court?

It gets worse in *Board Of Trustees Of Leland Stanford Junior Univ. V. Roche Molecular Systems, Inc.* Chief Justice worried about the word "of." Here's a fun snippet:

> That reading follows from a common definition of the word "of." See Webster's Third New International Dictionary 1565 (2002) ("of" can be "used as a function word indicating a possessive relationship"); New Oxford American Dictionary 1180 (2d ed. 2005) (defining "of" as "indicating an association between two entities, typically one of belonging"); Webster's New Twentieth

Century Dictionary 1241 (2d ed. 1979) (defining "of" as "belonging to").

As usual, the judge continues for several pages. Over "of."

The Law

As you can also see, there's a lot of regulation. I pasted the full extract of just this little tiny bit of part of the rules and official interpretation around reverse mortgages from one regulator to give you an up close to the tree moment so you can see the grain of the bark, feel the nubbliness, the many contours, and rich detail. The tree itself is far larger than just this little piece at eye level. It stretches up to the heavens, a canopy of lawsuits above and a pile of fallen branches of revision below.

The tree itself has grown from a small hillock of statutory law passed originally by the U.S. Congress. There's interesting geological formations within the hill of special interest agates and pork belly bones. It is a small hill, but in the distance through the haze above, you sense mountain chains of legislative process from around the world.

Now step back, you are in a grove of trees. Each as majestic and complex as the one we started at. The trees intertwine, there are regulations from multiple regulators. There's the CFPB we started at, the FRB (or Fed), the OCC, the CFTC, the SEC, then there are the individual U.S. states, some mere bushes, others taller than the federal ones. There are oaks, elms, sequoias, but also vines of consultant white papers, brambles of industry standards, and all-pervasive fungal tubes of law firm advice budding into mushroom caps of pleadings and strongly worded cease and desist e-mails. Did you know there is a single mycelium organism in Oregon over four square miles in size?

Zoom back further, the grove is just a dot in a forest. No, a jungle. The living, breathing bulk of not just financial law and regulation, but all of the law and regulation. Yes, you are a financial institution, but doesn't all the law apply to you? That new product that James in Capital Markets was talking about? The one financing dairy products? Are there laws about cheese? James wanted to do something international, where can you ship cheese? When? Who must you pay to hold your cheese? At what temperature? As if in a dream, you pause, click away to Google, and in the flutter of a lub of a half a heartbeat:

TITLE 21—FOOD AND DRUGS
CHAPTER I—FOOD AND DRUG ADMINISTRATION
DEPARTMENT OF HEALTH AND HUMAN SERVICES
SUBCHAPTER B—FOOD FOR HUMAN CONSUMPTION
PART 133—CHEESES AND RELATED CHEESE PRODUCTS
Subpart B—Requirements for Specific Standardized Cheese and
   Related Products
Sec. 133.146 Grated cheeses…

Maybe this applies to James' secured credit default swap rehypothecation tranched derivative exchange traded fund, maybe not, but you're going to have to check. It's not like James has any care, I mean idea, I mean he wants to be sure he doesn't go to jail over this, and he's relying on you.

And, not like you didn't know this before all my tree metaphor nonsense, there's a lot of law. So much law that it used to be used as a backdrop in TV shows like *LA Law* where they had bookshelves of law to let you know: hey, these actors, if they were lawyers, they would have had to *read all of that*. Today, we don't see the scale because it is hidden away behind our computer screens.

I have had the honor, privilege, and target drawn on my back of trying to assemble the full text of this law into a database for multiple financial companies. We found that the totality was something like two terabytes of laws and rules. That's just country and state level mind you, and not including municipalities, lawsuits, aka case law, industry standards, and so on.

Two terabytes doesn't sound like much in today's world. This isn't the early 1990s when I was threatened with "gigabytes" of data by a firm then known as Mead Data Central and now known as LexisNexis, one of the major legal publishers. Back then, a gigabyte was on the order of a thousand floppy disks and unimaginably huge and expensive.

Nowadays, you could put all the law on a thumb drive that's smaller than your thumb. It's less data than you probably have in your photo album—assuming you have over half a million photos. Maybe you do.

Now let's go back to the trees. Each pixel, every dot, on every one of those photos, that's a word of law. Don't hold me to the math because at this scale it doesn't matter. It's close enough. Knowing the law means knowing everything in your photo library and knowing who is related to who, and who that guy is in the background at the beach. And you don't know, and you don't even remember going to the beach.

There are two primary paths therefore for what it means to comply with the law.

Path 1: We'll send you your stuff in three days whether or not it's a Sunday or a holiday or you use a lunar calendar and worship Baal. In fact, we'll try to get it to you by tomorrow so that we never ever have to even get within spitting distance of violation of Reg Z. And we will keep meticulous records of everything we send you, when we sent it, and show how each word in the e-mail we sent you lines up with the requirements of Reg Z. And when a regulator comes and asks us, we can print out the spreadsheet for them. Heck, we have the spreadsheet sitting on a desk every day just in case a regulator decides to stop by. And there's flowers in a vase on the desk. Fresh flowers. Every. Single. Damn. Day.

Path 2: Path 1 sounds expensive. We'll hire lawyers when someone complains. Then, if it turns out it's cheaper to pay the fine than do path 1, stay the course—and, *hey, don't put that in writing.*

To sum up, the law is voluminous beyond belief, every single word can trip you up, there's no guarantee you have interpreted it correctly, or rather that your interpretation will hold up in court. You can choose to err on the side of being conservative and try to do "right," whatever that means, instead of just "legal" or you can throw caution to the wind. Obviously, the two choices aren't just two, there's a bazillion ways you can slice this baloney depending on your view of ethical behavior and, critically, of making money.

Making Sauerkraut From Cabbage, Aka Money, See What I Did There?

Money, no surprises, that's what this comes down to. Banking is boring. Holding people's money for them in a big metal box with a spinny ship's wheel for a door and giving it back when they ask is not very profitable.

It looks cool in the "getting the gang back together for one more job" scene, but that isn't really what Winthrop G. Winthrop III was going for when he started this thing.

The simple idea is this: Banks take deposits that they pay a little interest on, to attract the punters and their money, and then lend that money back out at a higher interest rate and turn the difference into jet skis. Maybe they do something else, but I am amusing myself thinking of Wall Street bonuses being paid out in personal watercraft.

Everything in Finance Is a Loan

If we are honest with ourselves, all of us have been, at one time or another, befuddled by the many terms in finance: Stocks, bonds, annuities, derivatives, credit default swaps, clothed or naked options, boils down at some point to this. The jargon is there, and I'm being more than half serious, to confuse you. Or rather to confuse everyone. Yes, there's usefulness in having a name for a specific thing, that's a ball-peen hammer for metal work, that's a framing hammer for, um, framing, that's a mallet for not damaging surface, and, my favorite, that's an engineer's hammer, aka baby sledge, for "engineering," aka smacking really hard. But ultimately they are things for hitting other things.[2]

Here's my list of financial hammers:

Mortgage = loan
Reverse mortgage = loan
Financing = loan
Credit = loan
Indebiture = loan
Hypothecation = loan
Rehypothecation = loan
Debt financing = loan
Bond = loan
Advance = loan

---

[2] Hammers have a second use: thumb locators. If you can't find your thumb, try putting a nail into a two-by-four.

Factoring = loan
Margin = loan
Revolver = loan
Line = loan
Deposit = loan
Liquidity pool = loan
Borrowing = loan
Loan = loan (just making sure you're paying attention)

You get the idea. Pretty much everything is a loan. One side of the transaction is borrowing and the other side is loaning. The borrower pays some amount, which may be called interest, fee, haircut, premium, point, coupon, share, option, warrant, equity, or something fancier, for the use of the lender's money.

Hold on, maybe you are saying, *my deposit isn't a loan, that's my money.* But it is a loan. You are loaning money to the bank. Makes you pause when you think about it that way? As a bonus, consider when the bank wants to give you a "line of credit" against your deposit. They are lending you your money. Instead of having to pay interest to you on your deposit, you pay them. Genius!

Back to Making Money

The challenge for finance is that all of these financial products, as they are known, carry risk that you or the bank won't get your or the bank's money back after loaning it out. Hey, risk, that sound familiar? Flip back a few pages, yep, there it is, market, credit, operational, and the subset of operational compliance risk.

The higher the risk, the higher the return, or larger the loss, at least most of the time. This is true for market risk, loaning money to subprime lenders means you can charge higher interest rates. For credit risk, you can charge cousin Louis, who doesn't have a good credit rating, an extra 4 percent on his car loan. For operational risk, it's a little different, you don't make more money, you save money as a bank. *Firewall protection for the data center? It's in a cement building, isn't that a firewall? Yes, funny, right? And no, I am serious, I'm not spending any more on computers.*

Compliance is a little different again. One aspect is, yes, saving money. *We have an AML department that checks a statistically meaningful subset of transactions for suspicious behavior every day and they are supported by a team of data scientists who train machine learning models based on the latest money laundering research and trends,* is more expensive than, *We have an AML expert who reviews two selected transactions a week.*

But compliance also allows for, *what if, and I'm just spitballing here, you know those class action lawsuits, like the ones against the tobacco companies, oil companies, and kids pajama companies, yeah those, plaintiff's lawsuits I think they're called, there's a zillion of those, right? Angela, you just got a thing in your e-mail about your cell phone battery; yeah, that's it, they take years and lots of money, and, you see where I'm going? The plaintiffs can't or don't want to wait years. We could pay them up front and then take over the case. I mean pay them a discount based on the risk that the case loses and something for our time and effort. Hey, we'd be the heroes here? Right? Getting the poor suffering plaintiffs money now against the big evil corporations? Jojo, go check with Legal and Compliance and see if they can interpret the rules so that we can do this. Angela, go find some plaintiffs who need our money, I mean help…*

By the way, yes, there is "structured settlement financing." That's totally a thing.

Notice that Compliance can be a competitive advantage in itself. If you figure out something that's potentially not illegal that everyone else isn't so sure of, you too can be a hero. Or, to use a more common phrase, Compliance can enable "financial innovation." And who doesn't like innovation? Your ability to innovate, however, may be directly correlated to the quality, quantity, and billable rate of your attorneys.

CHAPTER 3

How to Design a Compliance Department

I've covered the force pushing banks not to comply, namely it might get in the way of making money. What can be done? Regulation and fines and jail time is one thing, but that's after the fact and it's external. That's going to give us some nice scenes of people like Bernie Madoff in an orange jumper, but it's not going to do much for the ruinous impact of thousands of stolen life savings nor will it erase the decades of pool parties he enjoyed. Why do I always imagine water-related activities as the payoff?

Now, as surprising as it might sound, most bankers don't want to do bad things. It'd hazard the vast majority in fact. Sure they want to make money, but they don't want to do it by stealing from grandma or you or me any more than they want to get paid to punch people in the groin. People go to work every day in a bank just like they do in a restaurant. They don't want to poison people, they fundamentally do want happy customers. But the (please pardon me here) diarrhea keeps coming.

There's a couple of overlapping views of the problem, let's call them "the bad apple" and "the rotten culture." The bad apple is that one person who's doing all the law breaking, and the rotten culture is when the bad apple is in executive management, maybe even the boss. Evil can emerge from systems themselves without an "intelligent designer." Regardless, the bad apple analogy includes the spreading of the bruised fruit. One bad apple spoils the bunch and all that.

By the way, ethylene gas emission from a rotting apple does really cause the other apples nearby to spoil. I suppose the analogy in banking is a shiny new vehicle in the parking lot, with an equally shiny jet ski trailer, for the first bad apple inspiring the others. Or it can be just about survival for the other apples. When the bad apples are setting unrealistic quotas, the only way to keep your job is to inevitably slip into unethical behavior.

So how do you build a Compliance program that can detect bad apples, stop their behavior, and maybe even prevent them in the first place? One word: accounting.

Wait, what? I thought we were talking about compliance, and indeed we are. Accounting, like compliance, is both a concept and a department of people. I'm talking about the concept, which is the act of, um, counting. Instead of counting dollars, we will count controls and their effectiveness. And for all you accountants, you will understand already that good cash management is as much about good controls as anything.

What Is a Control?

When I was working at a certain global financial firm my department was on a high floor of a Manhattan skyscraper. One day, early in my tenure, and still very much unsure of myself, I went to the bathroom and then washed my hands. We were co-located with a former CEO of the firm who had an office and two assistants, because he was too old now for jet skis, I suppose, and he got perks of being treated like royalty instead. Which is important because the bathroom had elaborate, for corporate America, faucet handles.

Big, imposing, silvery shining faucet handles. Not as nice as the building down the street where the current CEO resided, but still, much nicer than would normally be there. This is important because they were not original equipment. This was not the "you get two seconds of water you filthy animal" at the turnpike rest stop. These winged beasts swung impressively. Till they got stuck.

I got one stuck under the spout. It would not budge. I pulled. Nope. I pulled again. It came loose. In my hand. Snapped off? I don't know. Water erupted from the open hole. Gushed. Exploded. There was a number on a plate on the wall, you know, the kind that says "If This Bathroom Requires Attention, Please Call." I called.

"Um, there's a water leak." *Note the passive voice. Remind you of any corporate announcements? I'm not taking blame. Also, the water was an inch deep on the floor already. This place had some good water pressure.*

"What is your name and department?"

I hung up.

I went down the elevator and told the security desk staff that I had heard there was a leak in the bathroom on the 46th floor, and then I left before they could radio maintenance or take down my information. It's not selling an auto loan with a balloon payment, but still, not my finest moment.

The faucet was part of a *control*.

A control is a process that mitigates risk. Taking an umbrella with you in case it rains. Locking your car in case someone wants your stuff. I had a single 20-pound cast iron dumbbell stolen from the trunk of a Saab 900 in 1995. I was exercising poor operational controls and the thief was a moron with one arm now longer than the other.

Just like with risks, there's a lot of ways to classify controls, and you can have a great deal of nonfun and spend a lot of time and money putting your controls into different piles. So with that in mind, here's a bunch of ways different people have come up with to think about controls. And while these definitions clearly overlap with each other that hasn't stopped people from making tests for Compliance, Risk, Accounting, Technology, and what-have-you certifications that require one to pretend these are as precise as a mathematical formula.

- Automated, a mechanized or, more commonly in finance, a computer application control. A time delay safe lock is an automated control. A web form that requires you to click "I agree," even though you have not read a single word of what you are agreeing to, is another.
- Manual, a person locking up the store or counting the money or asking, "Hey, what are you doing with that package of cash we are sending to the orphans?"
- Detective, a control that lets you know something may be up. An alarm is a detective control. "Hey, stop that!" It doesn't actually stop anything. My dog is a detective control. She will run around looking for a stuffed toy to alert me that someone is in the house.
- Preventative, a control that prevents bad behavior. Kinda right there in the name. A bear trap inside the cookie jar prevents cookies getting stolen. My dog is not a preventative control.

- Corrective, a control that not only stops bad stuff but also fixes it. A spell checker can be a corrective control. Not that I need on.
- Deterrent, something that deters bad behavior like a big sign that says "there is an alarmed bear trap in the cookie jar. Don't trust the dog, she's just hoping you give her one." And again, right there in the name. Did you not read the name first? Really, this is not rocket science.
- Output, a control that measures the output of a process. Checking the balances in the cash drawer at the end of the day and matching that up with what receipts say.
- Behavioral, training people what to do by directly telling them, um, what to do.
- Clan, norms of behavior often unwritten. For example, telling someone to paint the house, you would not expect them to paint over the windows. And as soon as I write this down I imagine someone painting the windows.
- Organizational, setting up the organization in a way that creates a control. A common approach is segregation of duties into different departments. For example, having a Compliance department that isn't part of the Sales group.
- Operational, a control that is part of a process. From my humble perspective, all controls are operational. But now I'm slipping into semantics and taxonomy. I do plan to do that about controls, but not here. Not now. No. I'm done with this list.

What's the point of all of these distinctions? Aside from an opportunity for someone to say in a meeting: *but that's a detective control, it's not going to do anything to stop the behavior.* And then everyone nods at the sage-ness and then goes about what they were doing anyway? Not much I'd wager.

Control Design and Effectiveness

You can't talk about controls without getting caught up in an argument about *design* versus *effectiveness*. You can't really talk about anything at a corporation without getting caught up in an argument, but that is beside the point. You will need to understand the difference between design and effectiveness because there will be a test later. Or at least testing.

Control Design

From a control design perspective, the valve is a control that keeps water in pipes when not being used and controls flow otherwise. The sign on the bathroom wall provides a second control mechanism should the valve or some other bathroom control fail, that is, *ewwww.* The security guard with a walkie-talkie was a third control.

A control is really the process, meaning me trying to turn off the water. A control point is the thing that enables the process, namely the beautiful but badly installed valve. Having multiple controls is known as *defense in depth.*

This particular defense in depth is via *Swiss cheese* control design, meaning that these controls weren't set up to stop all water leaks, but they were set up in a way that if a problem got through it might, sort of randomly, be caught by another control. Imagine a set of slices of Swiss cheese with each slice being a control and the holes being ways they can fail. If the holes line up, bad news. But those crafty Swiss and their gassy bacteria cause holes that are more random. So chances of getting past all the controls is reduced because, by design, they are overlapping at random. Taken together this is a *control environment.*

You can probably remember some event where a criminal caught someone "by chance." I witnessed one such event when some drunks were marauding down the street yelling and harassing people. One picked up a trash can and threw it into the street. NYC wire garbage cans at the time were very light and it bounced harmlessly off the hood of a passing car. It was a cop car.

The Internet calls this "instant karma." Google this and enjoy the videos. But it's not chance. The reason the cops were patrolling was exactly because defense in depth and Swiss cheese controls work.

Control Effectiveness

The faucet failed. It was not very effective. The rest of the control environment however *mitigated* the risk. Meaning it was overall effective.

If you were grading the faucet you'd maybe give it an F and all the controls together a B–. Or maybe you'd give it another grade. Let's have an argument. But save it, we have to get to risk assessment and testing, and before that we have to get to the pillars.

The Pillars of Compliance

Here we are, the top of the mountain, it's all downhill from here. The sky is clear, the wind is crisp. There, in the highest quality marble, is our Parthenon. The ideal compliance architecture. Each pillar is represented on some slide deck somewhere as an actual pillar because that clip art comes with PowerPoint. I'm not lying, I've seen this deck at every company I've worked in. Do an image search on "pillars of compliance." Look at that. So many buildings. So many fonts.

Are there three pillars or five? Seven or four? Maybe we can have 10. More would be too hard to remember. It can't be less than three, that's not going to hold up any roofs, and no slide can have just two bullets, that's more unacceptable than showing up for work in open-toed shoes, or fabricating customer accounts. I kid. But not really.

But Compliance, someone might point out, isn't an edifice, it's a process. It is eternal. It is a cycle that goes on forever and ever, building ~~viciously~~ virtuously upon itself. You could point out that PowerPoint also has circles and they are in SmartArt making them even easier than trying to put text boxes on clip art columns, but you don't have to mention that second part out loud. Do an image search on the "circle of compliance." Oh boy! Three, nine, twelve?

Or maybe, *clicks through SmartArt shapes,* a pyramid? No. Don't Google it. The slide deck is already at version 122. This way lies madness, or worse, a three-day offsite that is actually onsite in a basement conference room with fruit plates with too much melon. Please God, let's not.

At the risk of death by a thousand nitpicks and revisions, here are my pillars of Compliance. Forgive me.

- Policies and Procedures
- Training
- Testing and Monitoring
- Risk Assessment

Policies and Procedures

The average employee at giant bank was part of a companywide effort called "real estate rightsizing." Those with offices are moved to cubicles, those with cubicles have their walls moved in by a foot on each side, and everybody else is placed on long, open seating tables—to enhance communication, by allowing one to shout thoughts to co-workers without the difficulty of having to get up.

The GC, who I have been invited along to meet, however, has an office large enough to host its own conference table and a sofa. My boss and I sit at the table. The GC and his chief of staff are also there but discussing a different topic first.

"You have to read through the policies," the chief of staff says. "There's a policy review meeting and they say you have to note any objections."

"I hate policies. What do they really accomplish?" the GC.

A pause.

"I want to introduce you to the head of our policy office," my boss says, gesturing at me.

I smile, uncomfortably. It was not a good meeting.

But why did the GC hate policies? Probably because they often don't do what they are supposed to and end up exposing the bank to all kinds of litigation and regulatory action by saying things that the bank can't prove they are doing.

Policies and procedures are the bridge between regulation, management's *risk appetite*, and controls. Risk appetite being a fancy term for, *how close to the edge of what's ethical?* Take an example like insider trading. It's illegal to let bankers who are doing a merger deal between two public companies buy and sell stock in said companies. Or rather, it's illegal for them to buy stock because of information they have about the merger. And what about your other employees who know nothing of the merger? Or you? You're really not in the weeds of what's going on.

You could establish a *control room* to separate the *private* and *public* employees in your company and have them fill out paperwork about what they know and don't know and who they work with and are they related to anyone at the companies you invest in and blah-d-blah-d-blah. If you did that you'd need a fairly complex policy laying out all the procedures, which FINRA and SEC rules you're making sure are covered, and so on.

Or, you could say employees who work here can't trade individual stocks. Period. Full stop. Or, you could say employees just have to report any big trades they do. Or, you could say these people are adults, I will warn them about the SEC and FINRA rules and then I've done my job. It's on them. Each of these is a selection of risk appetite. Given the culinary feeling, think of it like a menu of scruples ranging from a cup of cottage cheese and celery sticks to a triple cheese burger with cocaine sprinkles.

An Aside About Policy Pet Peeves

Policies that say, *per Regulation W transaction with affiliates are limited…* Do you want me to read Reg W? No, you don't. You want me to read the company policy and do what that says. I should not be interpreting the law.

Policies that say, *you must also follow all related state and local laws.* And how would I know what those are? That's punting worse than the last season of *Lost. The meaning is up to you!* Bullshit. Just tell me what you want me to do and Compliance should know if the policy lets us potentially run afoul of Santa Fe's requirement that buildings downtown look like they are made of adobe—which is a thing.

An Aside About Congress

A funny aside about insider trading. If you trade on nonpublic information you can pay fines, civil and criminal, and you can go to jail for years. In 2022, Raj Rajaratnam from Galleon got $150 million in fines and 11 years in jail—although he was released to "home confinement" in 2019. Maybe you think that was too harsh, or you agree with Raj that he was the fall guy "for the feds' failure to convict any prominent bankers following the 2008 financial crisis." I don't know if you wept when you read his book, *Uneven Justice.* And we all know Martha Stewart, her patterned wool sweaters, excellent gingerbread houses, and dubious trading on biotech stock.

Martha Stewart Is Selling Replicas of the Nativity Set She Made in Prison is the title of the web page I copied this from.

Regardless, the rules I'm talking about are for mortals such as me, and again, I don't know about you, we've established that. But if you work at an investment bank, chances are you are required to preclear any trades before you make them. Some firms go so far as to simply prohibit any trading of named stocks by employees period. And you have to report all your accounts to the scarily named "Control Room."

While it may be true that most fines don't affect a bank's bottom line (see my other posts), it is true that nobody likes going to jail. You can't get your shirts dry cleaned, there is no view of Central Park from the lunchroom, and you are incarcerated. It's the last one, I think, that motivates people.

However, if you are a maker of the rules, like, um, Congress, then you didn't have to worry about knowing too much information when you bought and sold. It wasn't until the STOCK act of 2012 that U.S. legislators had to report their trading activity, even if there weren't a lot of limitations on said activity. And even now, years later, there haven't been anything like the financial and criminal penalties meted out to private individuals given to legislators.

Happen to have bought a lot of stock in the biotech company right before they have, say, an antiviral drug coming out during a pandemic? Well you did report it? No? You forgot to? But did file the paperwork after that mean article in the lamestream media? Well then, $200 fine for you buddy. I mean, that's totally hypothetical and I am not suggesting anyone Google "Kentucky senator stock act" or just "stock act violation." You're in Congress, you're the definition of ethical. Right?

To be fair, the SEC has brought one case against a Congress member, Chris Christie, and one against a former representative, Stephen Buyer. The settlement for Mr. Christie was:

> *The three defendants consented to the entry of final judgments that would resolve all claims and permanently enjoin them from violating antifraud provisions of the securities laws. Christopher Collins consented to be permanently barred from acting as an officer or director of any public company. Cameron Collins and Stephen Zarsky agreed to disgorge their avoided losses with prejudgment interest, totaling $634,299 and $159,880, respectively.*

Definitions of slap on the wrist may vary, so I leave it to you how severe being barred from being an officer or director of a public company and giving back the money earned through insider trading is.

As for Mr. Buyer, he made it under the wire. His indictment came a few days before I wrote this sentence and, if you are really alert, you will remember him from the list of SEC items in July. Well played sir, well played.

Just to put all our minds at ease, Congress is debating stopping all personal stock trading by representatives and senators, and they will continue, I'm sure, debating it. And I don't even need to Google.

I wrote the previous sentence in July 2022. It is now October 2022, and I read in the *New York Times* that "House Delays Vote on STOCK Act till after election." So, yep.

Back to policies and procedures. Here are my definitions, actual documents in the wild may differ greatly.

Policy is a document that describes *who* does *what when*. Ideally this is written as a "must" *policy statement* but could be a "may."

For example, bank employees must validate the identity of new customers in accordance with the KYC procedure. Or the board of directors may have a jet ski party once a year. The must policy statement is easier to audit because it was either done or not. The may statement does not have to be done, but Audit might still view it as a requirement and insist the board of directors get out there on the water.

Procedure is a document that describes *how* a policy is implemented step by step. How much detail do you need? That kind of depends. Pick up toothbrush, wet bristles, squeeze on toothpaste, brush teeth. We didn't tell you to put it in your mouth? You brushed inside your nose?

Policy and procedure are the direct connection to regulations. A good library of policies and procedures will list the regulations that they are trying to fulfill, note when each was last updated, identify who wrote the document and who approved it (who should be different from the writer), and be easily locatable by employees and regulators.

Maybe you're good with this. Maybe you are thinking, "but doesn't saying who does what when also have some amount of instruction? What's the difference between a policy and procedure?" And I say, "you're right" and "let's not have an offsite" because there is no hard-and-fast difference. Or for any other documentation about controls, including, but not limited to—which is a favorite get-out-of-jail-I-hope phrase in all policies—frameworks, principles, guidelines, specifications, run books, handbooks, manuals, instructions, desktop procedures, written supervisory procedures, and so on.

The difference is in audience, and is usually evidenced by size. A policy is for management to set the limits of behavior and should be short. Trying to prove to a regulator that your CEO read a 3-page policy is a lot easier than a 300-page policy. The other 297 pages are put in a procedure, which is for the people doing the work.

Meaning that you may well have 300 pages worth of instruction around a given topic, but you want to split it up in a way that it gets used and you can prove you use it. Make a document too long and risk the regulator or Audit department quizzing someone on a detail they never read. Make it too short and risk leaving out necessary details. A good policy and procedure set will be your best defense in a regulatory review. A policy and procedure set that sits on a shelf and is covered with dust from lack of use is your worst.

The key principle in writing any of these is that they not do not duplicate content. It's easy to cut and paste but let's say you have a policy statement "The credit department must review customer credit ratings annually." And then you copy that to a procedure. But then you have an epiphany that people are wonderful and underwriting reviews are expensive, so you make it an every-two-year review—or, please don't, you make it a biannual review and people have meetings where they argue whether that is every two years or twice a year, and I'm not saying I've had this meeting because I've had this meeting three times. But now the procedure is out-of-sync and maybe the procedure document text was copied into some training and some other documents and on and on.

Maintaining all these different documents is a challenge, and there's this one weird trick that can help, it's called, wait for it, a com-pu-ter. The problem is that Compliance departments are not great with technology because who becomes a Certified Compliance Professional? Not usually a programmer. The understanding of what is possible is therefore typically limited to Word and Excel without macros, PowerPoint, and maybe SharePoint in the sense of a shared file directory.

The result is that policies and procedures are written referring to each other. The policy on *AML* will mention that records must be retained for a period of time and that the *Record Retention Policy* needs to be read. That policy then has *Record Retention Procedures* that have the details about the various money-laundering record types—suspicious activity reports, customer details, and so on. And because customer details contain PII, there is a reference to the *Information Security Policy*, which probably links back to *Record Retention*. And so on and on.

In examining one policy at a firm I worked for—a 10-page policy on handling requirements for Regulation E on electronic funds transfers—it linked to 20 other policies, which linked to another 100 documents. Because all these other documents were connected via reference, they were, essentially, part of the original policy. The result is that to comply with the Reg E policy you had to comply with all of the other linked documents.

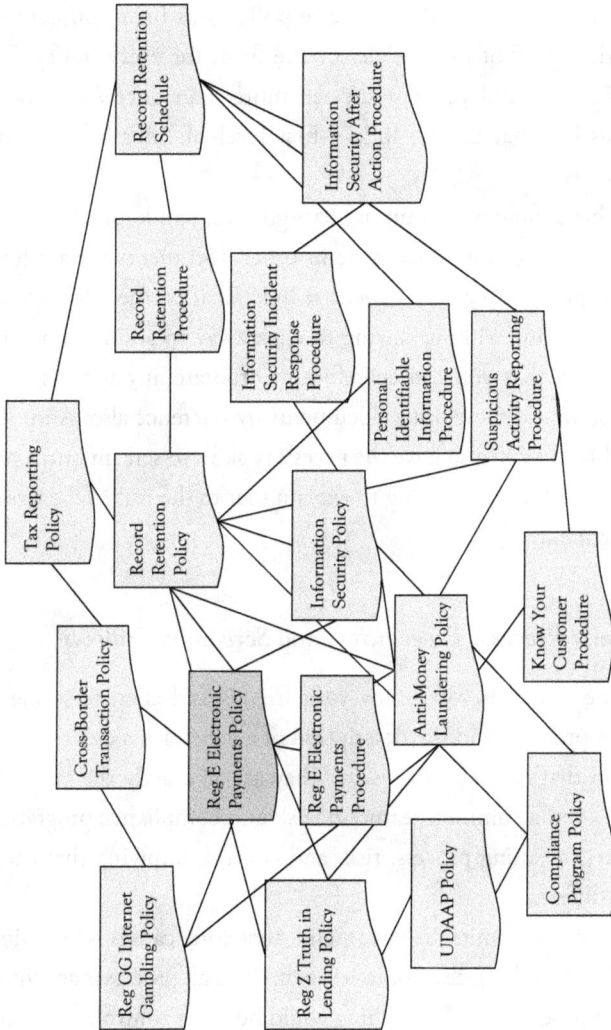

Simplified Reg E Policy Diagram

Fun, right?

Just going two levels of links deep was over 500 pages of material. There is no way that anyone was doing that, and therefore the entirety of the policy, which after following all the links to their ends or circular loops, would encompass most of the policy and procedure of the firm. Meaning: to verify that the one policy was being implemented meant auditing *all* of the policies of the firm, for every policy. That's ridiculous right? And yet, I witnessed more than once Audit departments insisting that all the links—first level of links at least—were being followed.

If you have some programming background, you know that you can incorporate parts of one document in other documents via a reference rather than just putting in a hypertext link. That is, the referenced text can show up inline without having to click away to another document. You also know that you can therefore incorporate any reviews, audits, tests, and so on, of these other documents by reference also. And, if you know all this you will also have the necessary skills to scream into a pillow when you get home after trying to explain that to the rest of the Compliance department.

Of Controls, Process, Procedures, and Screaming Pillows

Here's some info that will annoy your friends and alienate strangers: a control is a process. And the description of a control is a description of a process and that's called *a procedure*. They are all exactly the same thing. And yet ... yet, a common feature of risk and compliance programs is a PRC library, meaning process, risk, and control, implying that they are somehow different.

Every process limits behavior and therefore causes something to happen and something else not to happen. Thus all processes are controls. I suppose a process that did nothing could be not a control, so points for you if you have a process that does nothing.

If you've read this far, you'll recall my bathroom problem. If you've just skimmed and stopped here because of the subheading, shame on you. Go back, read all the words, and send a Facebook apology to your sixth grade reading teacher. She's on there you know. She's been breeding Angora rabbits. Weird, right?

One of the ~~stupider, less than useful~~, stupider things I've heard said, *a policy or procedure isn't a control because it doesn't stop anyone. I can put a sign on my daughter's door to not climb out the window to go see her boyfriend, but that's not preventing anything.* No, obviously, and what's going on with your parenting?

The sign is a statement of policy, which is the same as a definition of a control, which is the same as a documentation of a procedure. You could make it more explicit:

Policy: No one may use a form of egress outside of those authorized by parents at any time. All other ingress and egress forms must be locked at all times except in case of fire. I mean saying *don't use the window* would not seem corporatese enough.

Procedure: When entering or leaving the house, select either the front door or back door for egress or ingress. Grab handle. Turn … and so on. And stop sniggering at, *"back door."*

Control: No entrance or exit other than doors. Locks on the windows. Parents have key. Therapist contact info available when you turn 35.

Process:

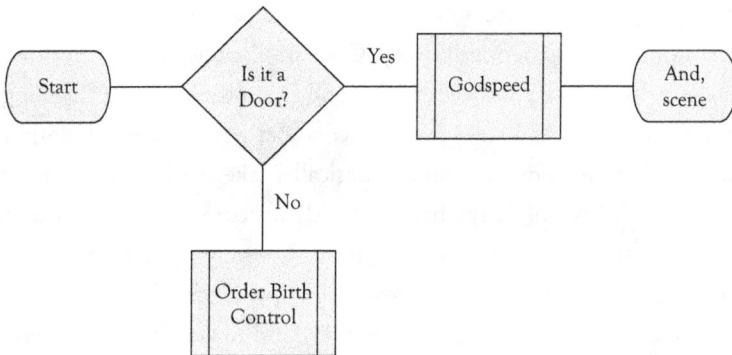

You could write this down in words in a Word document (policy or procedure), put it in a spreadsheet in Excel (control or process list), or in a nice diagram that someone spent way too much time fiddling with the box placement on (process flow). *Now that you have graduated with 16-plus years of education, you will be putting little boxes on PowerPoint slides all day long and then doing it again and again when someone inevitably complains that this line really needs to connect to that box. Welcome to corporate life.*

All of these different definitions cause definitive harm. People are literally compelled to write 10 different versions of how customer account information is gathered, but they shouldn't be. There's the policy, the procedures, the controls, the processes, the regulatory requirement, and so on. Over and over again, new documents are written with bits and pieces of others like some terrible library made of funhouse mirrors.

Then, because madness never ceases, the next step is to try to join back together what has been rent asunder by connecting all of this diaspora in yet another spreadsheet-cum-application-beast-to-feed known as a Governance, Risk, and Control (GRC) system. But more on that later. We have some pillars left before we get there. You may feel free to use your screaming pillow now.

Training

Training is the easiest to explain. It's training. A typical Compliance training regime will have some 20 to 30 courses covering topics such as Anti-money Laundering, Privacy, Code of Conduct/Ethics, Information Security, Operational Risk, Unfair and Deceptive Acts, Fair Lending, Transaction with Affiliates, Social Media Activity, Business Continuity, Antidiscrimination, and so on. Basically, take the list of regulatory penalties and lawsuits at the bank, sprinkle in recent trends in industry violations, and there's your *training plan*—a very important document you can show the regulators to prove you know all the things they have fined you for. Goodness knows it might be hard to keep track otherwise.

But why do we need training when everyone we've hired is an expert? I mean look at the resumes: *managed operational enhancement process in accordance with cutting edge regulatory submission requirements; designed, developed, and implemented next-generation financial risk framework approved by C-Suite; liaised with regulators, cross-functional matrix-based teams in a mixed-model global organizational structure...*

All those *adjectives*. Very impressive. Nonetheless, we need training because it serves a few purposes: it validates that people know the basics of the regulations; trains people on what the company's specific policies require; and checks a box that says "we have trained everyone on regulatory requirements, especially those we keep seeming to get wrong."

If you have ever been through Compliance training on financial regulatory topics you will know which it is. But maybe you haven't had the pleasure. Here's an example, including a knowledge check question to validate that you have been learned.

Anti-Money Laundering Training Excerpt

Start with a stock photo of two individuals, both of whom seem very animated in a very sunlit and modern office. Here's one I found:

Voiceover, and don't worry, you can turn off the voiceover and just get captions:

Elias has just met with a prospective new customer, Ms. Lydia Rodarte-Quayle, and he's concerned. He asks Armand for help:

The customer came in with three million dollars in gunny sacks stained with, I think, a lot of blood. She said she runs a dry cleaning business and that she often has to carry money in bloody sacks. Also she couldn't show me any form of ID other than a photocopy of a Rolling Stones concert ticket from 2005.

What should Armand advise Elias?

A. *Open the account. Money fits into sacks neatly, and it will make it easier to carry into the vault.*

B. *Open the account, but insist on getting the original concert ticket.*

C. *Investigate further personally. Follow Ms. Rodarte-Quayle out to the desert to visit her dry cleaning establishment. Don't tell anyone you are going.*

D. *Call Legal and Compliance.*

You think I'm exaggerating? I am most definitely not. Ms. Rodarte-Qualye was one of the cruelest villains that Walter White came across in *Breaking Bad.* She was ruthless, stepping over dead bodies…oh, about the test. Yeah, that's pretty much how the questions go.

Training will typically have an estimated time to complete, say 40 minutes, and the real game is how tricky the instructional designers can make it to find and press the "Next" button on each screen. Your any percent speedrun depends on fast reflexes and not getting distracted by reading the content. Or, you can just hide the course window behind your e-mail while the dialog runs on mute, and check back every so often to click "Next." This is why actual statistics of time spent in training tends to camel hump at a few minutes and hours. This statistic is never, ever, reported.

What is reported is completion percentage. And all banks are deadly serious about this. Whenever training rolled out at any bank I worked for, we would get regular reminders to press our teams to get "100% completion." I would be sent detailed spreadsheets of whoever had not taken the training yet and be prompted to reach out to them personally. Other than violations of information security, namely e-mailing documents to a personal e-mail account, it was the only management process so microscopic and comprehensive in implementation. If the CEO didn't do his training, and yes it's a man, there would be urgent discussions and obsequious but firm enforcement even for him.

Why so serious? Because training is a control—recall that all processes are controls—that applies to all of the regulatory-based policies of every bank. That control is as follows: *we told you what to do, so if you break the law, it's your fault.* Get it? The employee is breaking the law, not the bank. It's not systemic, it's the bad apple defense mentioned earlier.

We bribed the official of a small country's government we were issuing bonds for? And their family? And their friends? And their parakeet? Mon dieu! May we direct you to timecode 10:34:04 in the Code of Conduct training where it clearly says gifts must be less than $100 and to call this hotline if the employee thinks there's an ethical problem? On the one side you have employees thinking the whole training thing is a bureaucratic exercise with points for passing the training with the least effort possible, and on the other, the company readying the blame-shifting cannons in the event of trouble.

Of course, it is individuals who are doing any of the bad behavior, and sometimes, it is just one person, but in all cases, it is almost never that the criminal didn't know the rules. I'm not saying any banker could quote you FINRA rule 3220 (Influencing or Rewarding Employees of Others) from memory, that would be a very weird party trick, but everyone knows gifts can become bribery and there's some kind of limit on what's acceptable between a USB key fob and a gold plated hovercraft.

Here's an anecdote about gifts: bankers wanted to thank a Chinese billionaire for an enormous deal. They knew they couldn't do some fancy banquet or hire, erm, female entertainment, as was the custom in the *Mad Men* days of the 1960s. Or, as you won't be surprised too much, the year 2022.

April 13, 2022

After one of Switzerland's highest-profile corporate crime trials in decades, Zurich's district court convicted Vincenz, a former Swiss "banker of the year" who was charged with making millions through illicit deals while he was CEO of the bank.

Vincenz, who was acquitted on several counts, was fined 840,000 Swiss francs ($900,600) and ordered to pay nearly 1.6 million francs in damages [...] His lawyer told Reuters that Vincenz, who denies any wrongdoing, would appeal the verdict after he was sentenced to 3-3/4 years in prison.

Vincenz had told the court that a near 200,000 Swiss franc expenses bill for strip club visits was largely business-related, while a 700 franc dinner with a woman he met on dating app Tinder was justified because he was considering her for a real estate job.

Anyway, these bankers I knew were not looking to do that. They proposed a nice framed photo of the deal team and billionaire smiling for the camera. They had the frame purchased and a high-quality picture printed on glossy paper.

How much was the frame? asked the Compliance officer.
$100.
Ugh, that's the limit. Could you get a different frame?
Not in time.
How much was the photo?
$20.
Hmm. How about if you printed the photo out on a color printer at work instead? That would let us stay at the limit.

And so, somewhere in China, on a shelf, sits a photo printed out on a LaserJet of a banking team, a billionaire, in a nice $100 frame. See, people know.

In fact, the amount that employees at banks and, amazingly, all people know might surprise you: forging signatures is bad, using customer money to influence politicians is bad, opening accounts without consent is bad, issuing a mortgage to someone who doesn't have a job is bad, evicting a soldier who is at war from their house is bad, advertising an introductory low rate for a credit card and hiding the fee in 6-point font is bad, and accepting wire transfers from banks affiliated with North Korea is bad. Get Jimmy Kimmel to go out on the street and ask people these questions instead of *what's the capital of Maine?* and we'll see that people know a lot more about dubious ethics than they do about geography. Fun fact, I won a T-shirt at Sammy's Romanian Steakhouse for knowing it was Augusta. It was clear that Sammy had not expected to be handing out a free T-shirt.

As I've pointed out, there's a lot of interpretation and associated litigation on what the law means, and yes, there are cases where it's honest, or as much honest as you feel like thinking of honest, disagreement on details. I witnessed a case where the bank I worked for bought some bonds in a European country and arbitraged them in a novel way that rained money. But that windfall came from other banks, who hadn't noticed the opportunity themselves and they claimed foul. My bank said, *we admit no wrongdoing,* they never admit wrongdoing, *but in the interest of good sportsmanship,* and not pissing off all counterparties, *we'll put the money back,* because, frankly, it was only $100 million. Pff.

But in the main, the law and rule breaking by banks isn't in the details and it isn't because the employees don't know what they are doing isn't right. It isn't because they didn't take "training." It's because it was profitable to do what they did, until they got caught.

There may be one exception here, cryptocurrency, where people seem genuinely unaware of the law and believe that what they are doing is morally good. I have my doubts about the goodness and will cover crypto elsewhere, but I do not doubt that some people are convinced that it is the antidote to the evils I have listed. I may consider these people to be wrong, but their conviction internally is real and externally, only time will tell. Conviction, two senses of the word, and no, I am not sure these sentences will survive revision. Sentences! I did it again. I will stop now.

Did I ever learn anything from the many official hours and the actual fewer hours I spent taking my required training courses? Sure, I know some more about how complex Reg W and the definition of an affiliate transaction is. Did I ever learn something I didn't know about behaving ethically? No. And if I did, I am probably a risk to society.

Ultimately, the pillar of training is the *click to accept this agreement* of Compliance. Nobody reads it, it doesn't matter if they do because it moves all the onus onto the individual regardless, for the company the potential benefit of reduced penalties outweighs the cost, everyone does it, and it's still annoying as hell.

The information security researcher Bruce Schneier coined the term "security theater," which he defines thusly, "Security theater refers to security measures that make people feel more secure without doing anything to actually improve their security." Things like limiting liquids carried on planes, forcing passwords to be changed every so often, 90 percent of bicycle locks.

Security theater costs real money and time and aside from the potential to make people feel better and reduce litigation risk, it does, at best, nothing. At worst, it actually reduces security because it misses the real risk—bombs made onboard by combining water bottles of chemicals are not the likely attack vector, and frequently changed passwords leads to passwords that are largely the same with one digit incremented. Or causes harm—preventing mothers carrying bottled breastmilk.

Training is compliance theater. Bam. Mic drop.

Testing (and Monitoring and Auditing and Quality Control and Quality Assurance)

I'm tired of all of the overlapping concepts that people are hell-bent on being pedantic about their particular definition of, and I'm sure you are too, but now we are at Testing and the Gordian knot is at its thickest here.

Here's what the OCC has to say about this in the *Comptroller's Handbook* on *Corporate and Risk Governance* subsection:

> The CMS [Compliance Management System] should consist of the policies, procedures, and processes as well as the **monitoring and testing** programs that verify compliance with applicable laws and regulations and adherence to the bank's policies.
>
> **Quality control** provides assurance that the bank consistently applies standards, complies with laws and regulations, and adheres to policies and procedures.

Quality assurance is designed to verify that established standards and processes are followed and consistently applied.

An **internal audit** *program provides assurance to the board and senior management not only on the quality of the bank's internal controls but also on the effectiveness of risk management, financial reporting, MIS, and governance practices.*

So *monitoring* and *testing verify controls*—although no definition of the difference between monitoring and testing—and *quality control provides assurance of controls* and *quality assurance verifies controls* and *auditors assure quality of controls.* Super straightforward. It's regulatory Twister and I'm smelling someone's butt.

While I was always certain that these concepts were ill-defined, the actual act of cutting and pasting from the regulator's own muddled words surprised me. Nevertheless, you will find whole departments and organizations set up for each of these functions with their own policies and procedures and concomitant cross-group fighting over turf.

So now that we know these are all kind of the same, what is testing? It's pretty simple, make sure the controls are working, that is, control effectiveness. Open the faucet, water runs. Close the faucet, water stops. If the handle comes away in your hand, mark that down and buy new shoes.

The Risk Assessment

lasciate ogni speranza, voi ch'entrate
—Dante, possibly speaking about Risk Assessment

You are in a windowless conference room in a basement that you didn't know existed in your office building. There are miniature Danishes, with bright dabs of red and yellow jam; orange and green melon either too hard or overly soft; bagels, but not the good kind. There is cream cheese in small plastic tubs with pull off tabs that your fingertips can't get a purchase on. Burned coffee in giant thermos bottles slowly cooling off. Tiny napkins that absorb nothing. Paper plates you can't separate.

The chipper junior Compliance person encourages you to write your name on a tented piece of paper and take a seat, where a thick stack of documents, some with binder clips, awaits. Lunch will be at noon, you are told, you will not be leaving here today. Your day job, your mounting pile of e-mails, will be waiting when you return. You will be working the weekend, again.

You are here for the compliance risk assessment (CRA to which you can add P for, um, procedure?). You will be determining the likelihood and impact of the risk of breaking the law and the associated controls and residual risk.

The CRA will take into account other Compliance assessments such as anti-money laundering risk assessment, unfair and deceptive acts risk assessment, compliance skills assessment, and so on, which is where the stacks of documents on the table come in. They are called a *fact pack* and may contain those other assessments and some or all of the following: the company's risk taxonomy, the library of controls, a listing of all of the processes in your business, your policies and procedures, test results, audit findings, regulatory findings, training statistics, incidents, and issues. It's all this other data and your own knowledge that you will consider as you rate the risk of violating, for example, Reg F, debt collection practices.

You awake, the nightmare is over, but wait, you are still in the same windowless conference room. A different, but also chipper, Business Resilience junior staffer is handing out name badges. You have gone straight to the Business Continuity Risk Assessment. You are to assess the risks that might cause a disruption to the business, fires, sabotage, stupidity, angry gods, and so on. Again you will be working the weekend.

And again you awake: Technology risk assessment (TRA): The likelihood and impact of the risk of tech going down. Subassessments include privacy, information security, application health, technology staff skills, and so on. Finance risk assessment (FRA): Remember Sarbanes–Oxley aka SoX and associated controls and assessment from the turn of the century? It lives on here. HR risk assessment (HRRA?): The, blah blah, people, blah, risk, blah, controls, yada yada skills, and so on, yes it over-laps with the other ones. They all do.

It's assessments all the way down to the final circle of this particular hell.

The RCSA

The risk and control self-assessment (RCSA) is the annual, possibly quar-terly, or oh my God you poor soul, monthly exercise to come up with a view about risk in aggregate. You may pronounce it as "arr-see-ess-ay" or "rick-sah," and regardless, it will be further hours of your life that will never be returned to you, like watching *Avatar*.

RCSA is a pillar of operational risk. The thing to know is that risk assessment is a pillar for Compliance and it must join in with the larger company's RCSA.

I had glossed over the gory details before, so let's review what exactly a risk assessment contains.

R   The risks that face your business. This is your *inherent risk*. Calculate the *likelihood* of this risk occurring and the possible *impact* of such an incident.

C   The *controls* that you have that mitigate those risks and reduce the likelihood of impact.

SA   Assess, yourselves, the *design* and *effectiveness* of those controls. Then calculate the *residual risk*.

The goal is to figure out where you have the biggest risks and the weakest controls so you can fix them. The risk assessment is intended to also give you areas to focus on for training, testing, and staffing.

Here's the risk categories from the Basel II accords—more on them later—you can use them as a starting point for your own risk taxonomy arguments as discussed earlier:

Internal Fraud—misappropriation of assets, tax evasion, intentional mismarking of positions, bribery.

External Fraud—theft of information, hacking damage, third-party theft and forgery.

Employment Practices and Workplace Safety—discrimination, workers compensation, employee health and safety.

Clients, Products, and Business Practice—market manipulation, anti-trust, improper trade, product defects, fiduciary breaches, account churning.

Damage to Physical Assets—natural disasters, terrorism, vandalism.

Business Disruption and Systems Failures—utility disruptions, software failures, hardware failures.

Execution, Delivery, and Process Management—data entry errors, accounting errors, failed mandatory reporting, negligent loss of client assets.

As we start our meeting we will camera dolly into your face as we split the screen, Brady Bunch style, into memories of you at all those other assessment meetings. So many meetings.

Hang on, you plead, simultaneously from all your close-ups. *What was the point of all those tests, audits, incident reports, issue closure plans, and assessments? Why did we do them if we are going to have to look at all of this over and over again? Why so many assessments?*

Because, the chipper junior people from Compliance, Tech, HR, Finance, and Operational Risk assure you in simultaneous voices: the regulators require it. Here's the relevant section of 12 CFR part 30 aka Safety and Soundness Standards. Highlighting is mine:

1. *Role and Responsibilities of Frontline Units. Frontline units should take responsibility and be held accountable by the Chief Executive Officer and the board of directors for appropriately **assessing and effectively managing all of the risks associated with their activities**. In fulfilling this responsibility, each frontline unit should, either alone or in conjunction with another organizational unit that has the purpose of assisting a frontline unit:*

    *(a) **Assess, on an ongoing basis, the material risks associated with its activities and use such risk assessments as the basis for***

fulfilling its responsibilities under paragraphs II.C.1.(b) and (c) of these Guidelines and for determining if actions need to be taken to strengthen risk management or reduce risk, given changes in the unit's risk profile or other conditions.

2. *Role and Responsibilities of Independent Risk Management. Independent risk management should oversee the covered bank's risk-taking activities and* **assess risks and issues independent of frontline units.** *In fulfilling these responsibilities, independent risk management should:*

(a) *Take primary responsibility and be held accountable by the Chief Executive Officer and the board of directors for designing a comprehensive written risk governance framework that meets these Guidelines and is commensurate with the size, complexity, and risk profile of the covered bank.*

(b) *Identify and assess, on an ongoing basis, the covered bank's material aggregate risks and use such risk assessments as the basis for fulfilling its responsibilities* under paragraphs II.C.2.(c) and (d) of these Guidelines and for determining if actions need to be taken to strengthen risk management or reduce risk, given changes in the covered bank's risk profile or other conditions.

I love that paragraph 1 says "all" risks and paragraph 1(a) says "material" risks. What's the difference? How could you possibly include all risks? Like the risk the "?" key pops off my keyboard and I can no longer ask questions? I just keep mashing it back on. It's going to fall on the floor one of these days and the dog will eat it. Anyway, I would have been creamed for having such loose writing in a policy at a bank. But there go those regulators, the scamps, doing whatever they please.

Now for the word "independent." That's it. That's why you are eating your ninth presliced mini-bagel of the year. You, or I, might argue that independent assessment of risks could mean coming to your own conclusion based on the business' self-assessment. Or, one might argue, independent means having a whole separate assessment process for a specific functional area such as Compliance. I will let you guess which one every bank I've been at chooses, hint: it's in the following picture.

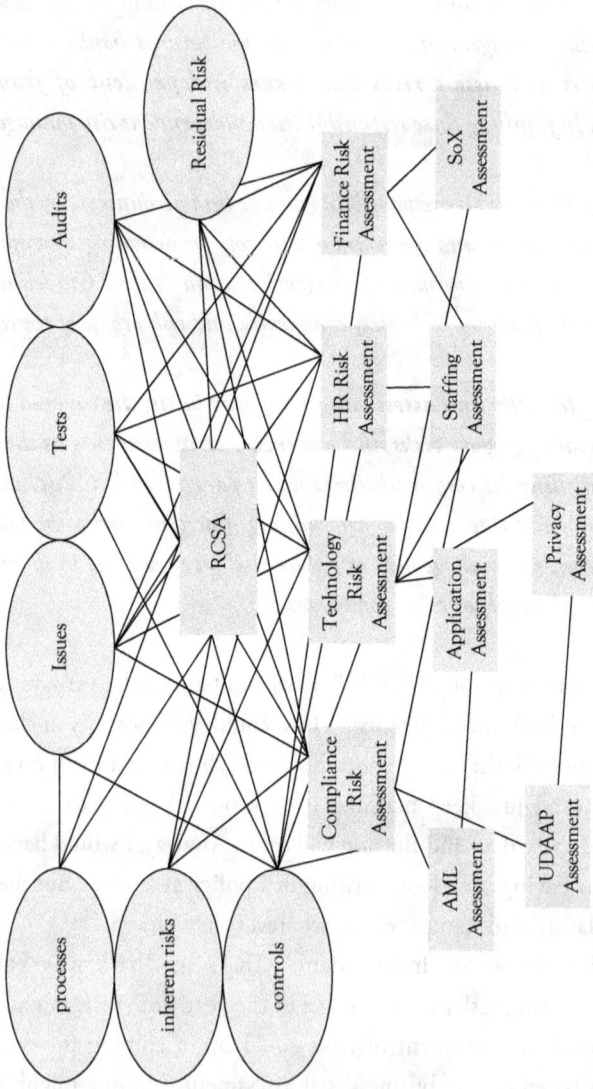

Simplified Risk Assessment Diagram

Why Is RCSA, CRA, TRA, and so on Stupid?

These risk assessments are a waste because they neither do what they say they will, assess risk, nor do they get used as they are supposed to for allocating people, time, and technology development. Moreover, because of all the meetings business people get fatigued and the data gathered becomes a check-the-box exercise—rendering it suspect. And lastly, the original purpose of the RCSA, in particular, capital reserve management, has been abandoned. Let's take each of these one by one.

Risk Assessments Doesn't Aggregate or Disaggregate—Spell Check Assures Me That's a Word

Assessing risks and evaluating controls is a good thing. I do it every day when I decide to floss even though I could just as well lie to my dentist. The problem comes about when you try to roll up data from lower-level risk assessments into a larger view or split apart a high-level assessment into smaller pieces.

Let's look at an excerpt of a potential RCSA for me in *heatmap* form—it's called a heatmap because red is, I suppose, hot, yellow less hot, and green is not a color of fire, unless you are burning toxic chemicals, and I think the analogy is coming apart.

My Personal RCSA/Aggregated Risk Assessment

	Inherent Risk		Control		Residual Risk
	Likelihood	Impact	Design	Effectiveness	Risk
	yearly monthly daily	<$1 $1 to $1,000 >$1,000	good meh no good	full partial weak	low medium high
Broken keyboard					
Hangry					
Poor fashion choices					
Killer bees					

The way I made this was by listing all the risks I face in the leftmost column. Then I check how likely they are to occur, what the impact will be, and then my controls to mitigate the risk and if they are designed well and effective. For each, I have to only choose one of three options, as indicated by the color-coded key in the heading row. Note: because this book is in black and white, the colors green, yellow, and red are represented by shades of light gray, dark gray, and black respectively.

I then calculate my residual risk. How? Well, I could say that I count how many reds or yellows or that I have a formula to logarithmically respond to the curvature or a multidimensional surface modeled on historical data captured over thousands of risk assessments. Or I could admit that I just kind of put a finger in the air and put what I feel seems right based on my feelings about this red, green, or yellow going to my boss.

In reality, companies set up some kind of equation for turning the data into a residual risk result, but then offer a "weighting" or "override" to allow for "subject matter expert judgment." Meaning: we put a finger in the air based on what we think will happen when the boss sees it.

In the abovementioned example, hungry-and-angry is my biggest residual risk. And it is true that when I haven't had lunch I am unable to think clearly and will possibly wear my clothes inside out or release the killer bees, which would be bad, mostly for me. These are killer bees, not trained killer bees.

But how would one aggregate my individual risks into a larger risk assessment for a larger group of people, say the city of Chicago where I live? I've seen people try to solve this by making a formula, as I had supposed for my own data. If there's more than three reds from a business then the aggregate is a red, or any red automatically made red for the parent, or yellow, or whatever. But the issue comes up of how this reads to management.

Politically no one wants to dismiss risks from business units or functions and at the same time, no one wants red. Red is supposed to mean, I need help to fix this, but it ends up meaning extra scrutiny, potential for firings, and that's not good.

Thus, the result of aggregation is 9 times out of 10 yellow. Here's how that might play out with some mini-bagels drying out on the table:

Hey, privacy risk is residual green, but we have that regulatory fine for that CD-ROM with everyone's name, phone number, and school mascot that went missing at FedEx.

True. Let's make that one red. Everyone concur?

Hang on, I own the privacy project. We've made a lot of progress. We're not done, but it shouldn't be red.

OK, put down yellow. What about the risk of killer bees? Audit gave us a satisfactory rating, but I know Larry is out after the "incident," so all good with yellow? …and the next 20 minutes will be spent arguing if we should have a less aggressive name for "killer bees." Maybe "aggrieved bees?"

Peer Pressure, Repetition, and Fear Leads to Known Results

The risk assessments are repeated from multiple angles: regulatory, technical, business continuity, HR, financial, and so on. This endless exposure to the overlapping, mostly the same data, and the associated concerns for how it might impact one's own work and bonus means no one will try to use an assessment meeting to introduce a new risk or point out a control weakness that was not widely known.

If they do try, they will quickly learn that no one wants to hear it. Most people want the meeting over and the silo-ed nature of these meetings drives away from open-ended discussion of how to improve the business to nit-picky "is it yellowish-red or reddish-yellow" analysis.

After all these risk assessments are completed, the areas of highest residual risk are, invariably, the areas where there are already regulatory findings or well-known operational losses. The same is true of RCSA, as it is of the CRA, the TRA, and so on. No one needed to have a meeting to figure that out.

Risk Assessment Does Not Allocate People, Time, and Technology

The stated purpose of risk assessment is to assure management and regulators that resources are aligned to improve controls and reduce risk where they are needed most. Turn those reds to greens.

It is true that staffing and technology plans are dutifully drawn up with references to the risk assessment results. However, as noted, the red areas are the ones where there's already fire, that is, regulatory issues, audit issues, or recent losses. If the toilet is overflowing, that's where money will be spent, and everything else will have to wait.

Which is to say, the risk assessment uncovers nothing new. How could it? If there were a risk that only emerged as critical as people poured through fact packs there would be far worse problems at the company—namely that nobody is talking to each other about anything ever. So unless you are running a company with a vow of silence, the risk assessment will end up confirming that the big issues are the big known issues. Yay!

RCSA to Manage Capital Reserves: A Forgotten Founding

Risk assessment, and especially the RCSA, were originally about banks trying to reduce the amount of capital reserves they needed to keep. When you deposit cash with a bank, the bank wants to use those funds to make loans and get interest income. It's what banks do. But they can't lend all of it out, even if that might be best for profits, because if people come to get their money out, and nothing's in the vault, that's a failed bank.

You need to keep reserves for all the risks. As discussed, those are, broadly, market (the whole market crashing), credit (deadbeats not paying you back) and operational. It is for operational risk that RCSA was created to lower the reserve requirement.

This approach took flight following Basel II, which is the middle of the three-part blockbuster of international banking accords developed by the Basel Committee on Banking Supervision (BCBS), based in Basel, Switzerland. Committee members include central banks and other banking regulators from around the world.

To belabor the metaphor, if you thought Star Wars galactic senate scenes were too pedantic to keep track of, allow me to direct you to the *Basel Committee on Banking Supervision International Convergence of Capital Measurement and Capital Standards* published in June 2004, page 149 of 251.

1. *The Basic Indicator Approach*

   649. Banks using the Basic Indicator Approach must hold capital for operational risk equal to the average over the previous three years of a fixed percentage (denoted alpha) of positive annual gross income. Figures for any year in which annual gross income is negative or zero should be excluded from both the numerator and denominator when calculating the average. The charge may be expressed as follows:

$$K_{BIA} = [\Sigma(GI_{1\cdots_n} \times a)]/n$$

Where
K_{BIA} = *the capital charge under the Basic Indicator Approach;*
GI = annual gross income, where positive, over the previous three years;
n = number of the previous three years for which gross income is positive;
α = 15 percent, which is set by the Committee, relating the industrywide level of required capital to the industrywide level of the indicator.

Let's take a moment to feel bad for me for having to figure out how to type that equation in because it didn't cut and paste from the PDF. It does look pretty cool though, right? What does it mean? It says that banks have to keep 15 percent of their gross annual income, averaged over the past three years they didn't lose money, in reserve for operational risk losses, which includes all the things I copied and pasted above and again here so you don't have to flip pages: misappropriation of assets, tax evasion, intentional mismarking of positions, bribery, theft of information, hacking damage, third-party theft and forgery, discrimination, workers compensation, employee health and safety, market manipulation, antitrust, improper trade, product defects, fiduciary breaches, account churning, natural disasters, terrorism, vandalism, utility disruptions, software failures, hardware failures.

Oh, and also, per footnote 90: *Legal risk includes, but is not limited to, exposure to fines, penalties, or punitive damages resulting from supervisory actions, as well as private settlements.* Zoinks!

The 15 percent is a lot of money. If you are a big bank that might be hundreds of millions of dollars that you still can't lend out for those sweet, sweet interest payments and just sit there in the vault, playing canasta, or whatever hundreds of millions of dollars do sitting in a vault.

What's that Mr. Banker? You aren't like all the other banks? You aren't as risky with your safe and boring business? Well, worry not! Basel II has you covered with:

2. *The Standardized Approach*

652. In the Standardized Approach, banks' activities are divided into eight business lines: corporate finance, trading and sales, retail banking, commercial banking, payment and settlement, agency services, asset management, and retail brokerage. [...]

The total capital charge may be expressed as:

$$K_{TSA} = \{\Sigma_{years\ 1-3}\ max\ [\Sigma\ (GI_{1-8} \times \beta_{1-8}),\ 0]\}/\ 3$$

Where

K_{TSA} = *the capital charge under the Standardized Approach*
GI_{1-8} = *annual gross income in a given year, as defined previously in the Basic Indicator Approach, for each of the eight business lines*
1–8 = a fixed percentage, set by the Committee, relating the level of required capital to the level of the gross income for each of the eight business lines. The values of the betas are detailed as follows.

Business Lines	Beta Factors
Corporate finance (β_1)	18%
Trading and sales (β_2)	18%
Retail banking (β_3)	12%
Commercial banking (β_4)	15%
Payment and settlement (β_5)	18%
Agency services (β_6)	15%
Asset management (β_7)	12%
Retail brokerage (β_8)	12%

That took even longer to retype. There was a !#@% table! What does it mean? It means not every kind of business requires 15 percent operational capital reserves. Retail banking is safer—remember this is 2004—so only 12 percent there, but wildcat corporate finance is higher at 18 percent. You win some, you lose some.

What's that Mr. Banker? You would never ever ever ever have *misappropriation of assets, tax evasion, intentional mismarking of positions, bribery, theft of information, hacking damage, third-party theft and forgery, discrimination, workers compensation, employee health and safety, market manipulation, antitrust, improper trade, product defects, fiduciary breaches, account churning, natural disasters, terrorism, vandalism, utility disruptions, software failures, hardware failures*—or legal fines and settlements? Oh, and you have all kinds of smarty-smart pants on your payroll who have no trouble typing facing equations all day long? Well, it is 2004 and you seem like nice people so, let me introduce: *Advanced Measurement Approaches*, please hold your applause until I've typed up the full equation.

Let's return to the Basel committee:

3. *Advanced Measurement Approaches (AMA)*

655. Under the AMA, the regulatory capital requirement will equal the risk measure generated by the bank's internal operational risk measurement system using the quantitative and qualitative criteria for the AMA discussed as follows. Use of the AMA is subject to supervisory approval.

And then several densely written pages later:

Business environment and internal control factors

676. In addition to using loss data, whether actual or scenario-based, a bank's firm-wide risk assessment methodology must capture key business environment and internal control factors that can change its operational risk profile. These factors will make a bank's risk assessments more forward-looking, more directly reflect the quality of the bank's control and operating environments, help align capital assessments with risk management objectives, and recognise both improvements and deterioration in operational risk profiles in a more immediate fashion.

But, surprise, there is no equation! Or rather, there's a bazillion, but those are all stashed away in the bank. Here are some graphs from a presentation by a JPMorgan Chase employee to the Boston Fed from 2005. A fat-tail log normal graph based on statistical best fit. Super-duper. Are you not impressed?

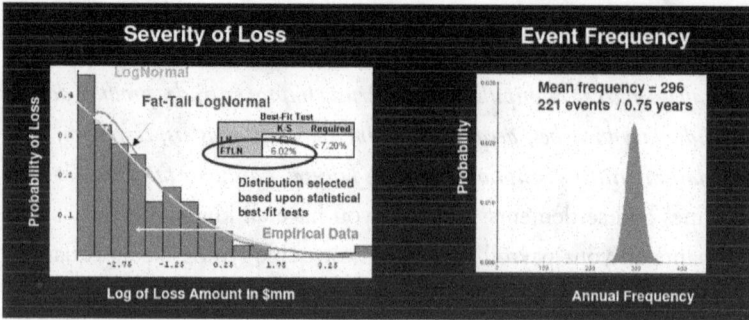

All of this boils down to a much simpler albeit still lengthy statement. If, Mr. Banker, you don't want to hold 12, 15, and 18 percent of your capital for a rainy day, gather some data about rainy days of the past few years, hold some meetings where you talk about the chance of rain in the future, aka scenario modeling, throw it all in a Cuisinart of mathematical ~~gobbledygook~~, modeling, to estimate what you might have to spend when it rains.

And then, you can discount that rainy day fund based on having a strong set of controls. How do you and we know they are strong? Well, how about a risk and control self-assessment? Bingo. There it is. The reason big banks were willing to spend literally hundreds of millions of dollars on people and systems to gather risk assessments and mush them all together into an overarching RCSA. It might allow them to free up some of that cash they were bound by regulators to hold on to.

Banks worked hard doing "parallel run" for years with the standardized approach in effect while they tried to prove to regulators that their AMA models were solid. A few finally got the OK, JPMorgan Chase, Citigroup, and so on.

And then it rained. And rained. And the mortgage crisis was far larger than any past rainy days had been. It was beyond what any scenario session had imagined. It didn't care about anyone's control effectiveness rating for *Regulation J: Collection of Checks and Other Items by Federal Reserve Banks and Funds Transfers through Fedwire.* It blew up all the fancy math.

Thus, Basel IV, a New Hope, is considering SA, aka, standardized approach, when it comes to theaters in 2023. There's plenty of wrangling among risk experts about how SA is going to force banks to have to put even more cash in mothballs, but don't expect anything to happen anytime soon.

Here's the first kicker related to the AMA or SA or any Basel require-ment, in the committee's own words: *The standards established by the accords are voluntary. The BCBS has no enforcement powers but relies on each participating nation's regulators to implement them. Regulators can also impose more stringent standards if they wish.*

Meaning: Each country's regulators have to look at the proposals and make their own rules, if at all, and that takes years and has allowed juris-diction shopping.

And the second kicker, as noted, the mortgage crisis revealed what everyone knew, the models were built on sand.

And the third kicker, RCSA was only ever an adjustment at the tail end of AMA, which was mainly about past events and future guesses.

And the final kicker, AMA, with all the analysis, specialized staff, meetings, software, didn't save much, if anything when all was said and done. Most banks don't use it and for those that do it is not at all clear that it has been a benefit. It certainly hasn't reduced their regulatory penalties.

RCSA was never worth it. But banks are creatures of habit, and it's a lot easier to stand up a process than pull out a pole that nobody is quite sure if it's the one holding up the tent. And so the windowless rooms hum with the shuffling of fact packs and mini-bagels continue to split, but never in the middle where the cut is, but sort of halfway with one part hanging. The inferno is eternal.

CHAPTER 4

A Perfect World or Why Compliance Hasn't Been Solved With Software

In concept, all the pillars of compliance are supposed to work together efficiently. Is it possible? Yes, but it happens only rarely. You will not be surprised that yours truly has been part of one of those fleeting moments—only to watch it get eroded away by the sandpaper of corporate friction.

Let's start with a success first: It was in business continuity, which used to be called *disaster recovery*, but that sounded too negative. Business continuity is typically handled by Technology Risk departments and not Compliance because the main thing in a disaster, at least from a company's point of view, is getting the computers back online. And getting employees to safety. Of course. Yes. But then the computers—they make the money happen.

Regardless, the structure of business continuity compliance is the same as any regulation, such as Reg A, exemption from registration for public offerings, and will therefore serve our purpose of examining a well-oiled compliance program.

Quick aside, when I cut and pasted the name of Reg A from the SEC website, I accidentally got this picture that was on their website. I'm not sure why a woman with a microphone talking to a group of people who seem happy to be getting paid to sit in a photograph for the SEC is relevant.

Maybe she is convincing them that she should have to register for a public offering, and they are like, "hey, we're just here for the $75 and the free cookies, do whatever you want," and the SEC is kind of saying that's how the rules work, you only get in trouble if you aren't paying out the money and cookies? Like, we won't regulate ponzis like Madoff and cryptocurrencies like Terra/Luna unless enough "regular" people are losing money. Nah. Couldn't be. I'm just reading way too much into some stock photo. Anyway…

(Not Strictly a Pillar, let's call it the Foundation.) The Law. Let's look at what the rules for business continuity are: primary regulations and industry best practices.

Primary regulation: The *Federal Financial Institutions Examination Council (FFIEC) Information Technology Examination Handbook (IT Handbook)* includes a handbook on business continuity. The FFIEC members include the Board of Governors of the Federal Reserve System (FRB), the CFPB, the FDIC, the National Credit Union Administration (NCUA), the OCC, and the State Liaison Committee (SLC). Exciting stuff!

And you're already stopping me because you are aware that the FFIEC IT is not law or rule, it is *guidelines*, but what does that mean? According to a footnote on the FFIEC website: *Each FFIEC member agency may use the principles outlined in this booklet, consistent with the member agency's supervisory authority.* Well, that doesn't help.

Back in the section on the law, we talked about how the meaning of the law is fuzzy. Well, this cuts both ways. The regulators can also take interpretation on their side, and in the case of FFIEC, it is functionally a regulation even if it technically isn't one. This means one of those member groups, the Fed, FDIC, OCC, CFPB, and so on, can issue a cease-and-desist order, a penalty, a requirement to stop adding assets, a firing of a board member or executive, or even take away your banking license. So ignoring the FFIEC handbook is equivalent to ordering the fugu from a trainee sushi chef on the risk appetite menu.

Industry best practice: The Disaster Recovery Institute International (DRI, what happened to the last I? I don't know) issues industry standards and provides certifications for business continuity professionals. I was once a Certified Business Continuity Planner (CBCP) and Certified Information System Security Professional. Hold your applause please.

These are even less official rules than the FFIEC guidelines. However, abiding by industry common approaches makes it easier for the regulators and regulatees—which is not a word—to agree about how to do something that's open to interpretation, which, as we've seen, is everything. Having most of your business continuity staff be CBCPs, which makes everyone more comfortable that you've got your act together. And the fact that DRI, ISC2 (strangely not an acronym anymore), Project Management Institute (PMI), and a bunch of other acronym industry groups that are accredited because they say they are, get paid for providing courses and annual fees. That's just a fortunate side effect.

Now that we have the rules in place, we can write a policy.

Pillar 1. Policy and Procedures

The policy takes each major requirement from the regs and industry standards and morphs them into policy statements that identify *who* will do *what when*. As an example, *All business units must perform a business continuity risk assessment annually.* That makes each policy statement a high-level description of a control. And, bada bing bada boom, you have those mini-bagel meetings ready to get scheduled. (See risk assessment for mini-bagels if you have not been following along.)

We had only a dozen policy statements, and they were all this clear and concise, making it easy for executives and regulators to see the scope of the policy quickly. And I've got nothing snarky to say about that. A concise, clear language set of statements really is a good thing for everyone.

Next, take each of those statements and expand it into a paragraph or two to add more detail. One standard for each policy statement. For example, *Business continuity risk assessments must include a list of all computer systems used by the business and a recovery time objective for how quickly they need to be restored in the event of disaster.* The standard also includes key metrics, for example, *the percentages of computer systems requiring recovery in less than an hour, less than a day, and longer than a day*. Taken together, the policy statements and standards are the company's laws.

Now we write a set of procedures where the content, critically, again can be matched one-to-one against the standards. The procedures are where we put all the details that a regulator or auditor wants to see. How many days to wait to send an e-mail after a disaster, the font for the disclosure, the kind of burlap to be used for the sacks of money if the safe was blown up, and so on.

After the procedures were done we created forms. Literally forms in Microsoft Word with underlines and checkboxes where each procedure step had a corresponding item on the form. We didn't expect people to fill these forms out, instead they were used to design a computer application that automated implementation of most of the policy. Anyone doing the business continuity risk assessment or looking for a report with the metrics just used the system.

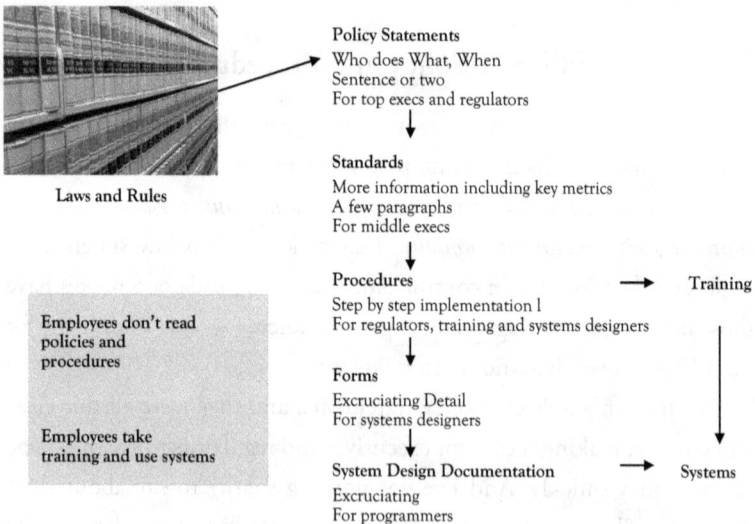

Laws and Rules

Employees don't read policies and procedures

Employees take training and use systems

Policy Statements
Who does What, When
Sentence or two
For top execs and regulators

↓

Standards
More information including key metrics
A few paragraphs
For middle execs

↓

Procedures   →   Training
Step by step implementation l
For regulators, training and systems designers

↓

Forms
Excruciating Detail
For systems designers

↓

System Design Documentation   →   Systems
Excruciating
For programmers

This approach has some direct benefits as follows:

Information is sorted by audience and their tasks. Executives review and approve policies to decide the firm's risk tolerance. They don't need to know how to perform an "after action review," but do need to know that the policy requires review of what happened after a disaster—which is reasonable.

Information is not duplicated. Because detail is segregated in this way, there is no duplication between the layers of the documents. Duplicated information is harder to maintain and with this structure, people know where to look for information.

Traceability. There is clear traceability from laws and rules to computer systems that enforce the company's controls for those rules. This means that the bank could tell the regulator: "Here's the rules you gave us, here's our policy, and here it is all the way down to the computer code that enforces our compliance."

All of this leads to an outcome you already know—because you read the picture first—employees don't need to and shouldn't read policies. As I said earlier, requiring staff to read policies is passing the buck on responsibility to ensure compliance. Relying on people to digest hundreds or thousands of pages of policy and procedure all but guarantees noncompliance.

Policies and procedures are technical documentation for the operation of the company. They are not intended for the hoi polloi to understand and implement. The enforcement of policy is through that automated system that only allows for business continuity risk assessments to be done in a way that matches the forms, that come from the procedures, that tie to the standards, that match the policy statements, which link to the regulations.

An analogy would be a door in a building. You don't need to tell people to use the door to enter and not through the walls. That is solved by the electrical repulsion of valence electrons in matter, that is, physics, that is, you can't walk through walls. The business continuity policy system was just such a door and wall.

Pillar 2. Training

Are you being snarky already? Are you going to suggest that *people might go through the windows*? Well no windows in this building then. *Well, what if people try to drive a car through the door? Or a cow? Then your business continuity system will be full of cow shit*. Fair enough. People will do almost anything. Thus there is a need for the next pillar: training.

Training is for managing the controls that can't be automated, and these are largely about understanding concepts and any place where there's an unstructured data field aka a fill-in-the-blank section. This is much like an essay question on a standardized test. The computer has no problem with checkboxes or radio buttons, simple choices. However, "free form text" entered by users can, and will be, of all levels of quality. This is equivalent to a blue book where an eighth-grader's desperate answer to "primary causes of the French Revolution" might be: *They were offered cake, but they were French and did not like cake.* Or, they might just draw a hat.

Thus, training should be considered a last and desperate step. In our case, we looked hard at every free-form text field. For example, critical business systems, such as the ATM network, needed to come back online quickly after a disaster. Customers, I am told, get antsy when they can't get their money. Which makes regulators antsy. Both of which are bad. However, the application that prints monthly reports on cafeteria usage is not as critical. This seems obvious, but leaving it to the wisdom of the employee filling out the risk assessment is akin to having a door with no wall around it.

We didn't provide a text box to write in, "Why is this application critical," instead we had checkboxes for *how many customers use the system, how often,* and so on. What would have been even better would have been if we could have linked directly to usage data about the ATM network and cafeteria system, but that would have required some cross-business-silo magic that we did not have the corporate mojo for.

Regardless, there is still going to be some need for training, which, in this case, we did by directly linking the training to the procedure steps and focusing the training on the use of the automated system. Again, we could show the direct path from regulation through policy statements, standards, procedures, training, and computer application to compliance. That through line made both the testing and the software more robust.

Pillar 3. Testing

Testing business continuity meant two things: first, testing that disaster recovery plans would work (people get away from the fire, for example) and second, testing the program itself—by which I mean, test all the stuff I'm writing here: the policy, the procedures, the standards, the training, and so on.

Test the Plans

The testing of each business' recovery plans was one of the policy statements, standards, and so on—and it is a standard that lays out key metrics, such as *number of tests performed and number of tests that completed successfully*. A recovery test, by the way, might be done by switching off the main server and seeing if it fails over to a backup, or just falls over. The next part of the test is to turn the main server back on and see what happens—smoke, fire, and quiet computer humming. So when the technology help desk tells you to try turning it off and back on, you can be reassured(?) that this is state-of-the-art testing for massive data centers also.

As an interesting aside, remember when I said ~~computers~~ people first in a disaster? Well, if there is a fire, computers tend not to like water, so sprinklers are a no-go. Fire suppression in data centers therefore focuses on a different leg of the fire triangle—heat, fuel, air—by getting rid of the air. It's safer for the technology, but less safe for the people who, on the whole, enjoy breathing. This is not something you want to be around when it goes off, and a reminder that the computers make the money.

Test the Program

Enough frivolity of flammability—the testing of the overall program is far less fun, but you didn't get into Compliance for fun—and if you did, you are one strange duck. Nevertheless, the same linkage from laws to policy to yada yada yada provides an exact roadmap for auditors and regulators to know that the program is designed to meet regulations.

The second component of a control, after design, is effectiveness. In our case, all the metrics we laid out in the policy were exactly the metrics required to show that the program was working. Thus, testing of program effectiveness was just a review of the metric reports.

Thus, overall testing of the business continuity program was, as it should be, quite boring.

Pillar 4. Risk Assessment

Risk assessment, like testing, has two components. The risk assessment for how bad a disaster would be—which dovetails with the development of appropriate business continuity plans–and the risk assessment of the overall program.

We've already covered some of the bits about business continuity risk assessment via the policy, procedure, and so on. It is absolutely, as noted, a mini-bagel exercise and there is much that can be done to make it more streamlined by not requiring repeated gathering of the same data from the business, but again, not enough corporate mojo for us to go beyond our remit to solve for business continuity, which we did as well as we could.

The good stuff is the risk assessment of the overall program. There isn't one. Or rather, it's the same as the testing of the program, which is just looking at reports of metrics that were laid out already in the policy. This is because testing and risk assessment have the same inputs and outputs. The input is the set of controls and the output is the health of those controls.

In our "perfect world," the control evaluation data is already there and we can map it automatically into a risk assessment, no need to duplicate or stuff people into windowless conference rooms—which do not have oxygen-depleting fire alarm systems, but are still a hazard to consciousness.

What Became of the Perfect World?

Over time, the original 8-page policy became 10 pages, then 15, then more than 20. The discipline of "who does what when" was not adhered to and some policy statements were written as "may" rather than "must"— turning audits and regulatory exams into interpretive dance instead of simple "did you do the thing." Procedures began to duplicate content from the policy out of fear that people wouldn't go look at the policy. Training expanded and contracted based on concerns from the business about how much time they had to spend on training. And the system fell out of precise sync with the policy and procedure.

In short, utopia was no more, and it became just another corporate program like any other with gopher holes and a leaky roof caused by maintenance and changing management who had either forgotten or never understood the careful interconnection between the pillars.

And who can blame them? The program architecture was done by hand and I, and others, had spent countless hours weeding out repetition between documents, adhering to specific vocabulary use, cross checking any change across all of the program. All the while I would be asked, *Do we have to?* and be told *You're such a nitpicker.* For goodness sake, I had a manual of style and usage longer than the actual policy that specified, among other things, acceptable fonts—Arial 10 point, sadly corporate insisted; the punctuation of bullet points—no semicolons, you freaks; and the number of spaces after a period—one, always one, did you learn to type on a typewriter or something?

It wasn't a failure of the people who inherited the pristine garden of business continuity, it was that we had to rely on manual controls—sounds familiar? Manual controls always tend toward breaking down. First the little stuff, then the bigger items. People get tired. They forget. They just want to tweak *this one thing*. It's preventative and not glamorous to stop the rot and push back against *the one thing*, and the work doesn't get rewarded. It was and is, plainly, a pain for everyone.

Why Don't Governance, Risk, Compliance (GRC) Systems Work?

I need to ~~complain~~ expand a bit more about how banks currently collect and manage compliance data. And to do that we must discuss what data and information are and how they are used and useful, or not.

As you have seen, I like to draw pictures with lines and text boxes. It's a defect of my character, but it's too late for me to change, only to embrace it. In that spirit, here's how information works:

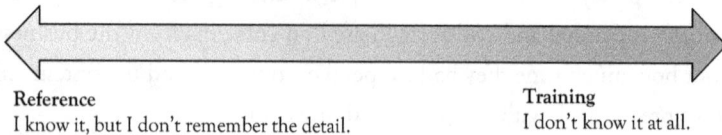

Reference
I know it, but I don't remember the detail.

Training
I don't know it at all.

If I need to put air in my car's tires and want the correct amount, it's a reference activity to be reminded for the thousandth time that it is 32 pounds per square inch in all the tires. If the tire pressure monitor continues to light up anyway, it is a learning activity that my tires are so old they won't stop leaking—a slightly less than $1,000 learning activity as it turned out. All information falls somewhere on this continuum. That's why I used a gradient. It's a continuum.

But what if the design and organization of the information doesn't align with how I need to use it? Now I get to use two axes, but sadly no gradient.

Taking a three-hour training course to find out my tires need 32psi would be boring and a waste of time. I also might miss the part where they say 32psi because I was staring out the window. Similarly, a graph

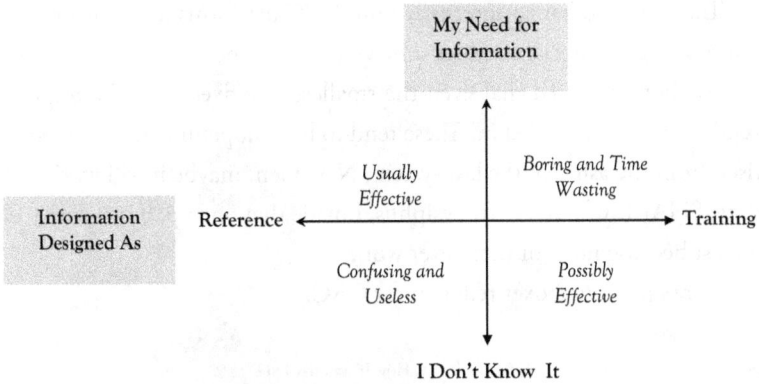

of vulcanized rubber elasticity versus time and conditions would do little to tell me that old tires can't form a seal against the metal wheel. It's a cool graphic for sure, but there is no way it's going to stop me from being stranded on the side of the road on the New Jersey Turnpike.

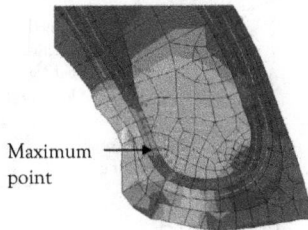

A. Normal tire bead

Let's put this in the context of Compliance and the information from all those pillars: assessments, audits, regulations, issues, policies, and procedures. These seem like the kind of thing you'd want to keep in a computer. Plenty of vendors agree with that view, and the result is a technology market for GRC systems.

IBM OpenPages, RSA Archer, MetricStream, ServiceNow, Nasdaq BWise, AuditBoard, ZenGRC, OneTrust, and many others range from enormous global behemoth systems that do everything for everyone to nice applications for payments or information security. All, however, except for Archer, are mandated to have BiCapitalized names.

There are also banks' internally built GRC platforms that may or may not have a commercial product somewhere at the bottom, but have been so heavily customized that even the smallest bug fixes from the original vendor cannot be loaded in. These tend to have hopeful names: Phoenix, risen from the ashes of the last system; Next Gen, maybe it will work this time; SHARP, which it isn't; Sysiphus, I made that one up, but it does feel honest because none of them ever work.

Here's my four-boxer redrawn for GRC.

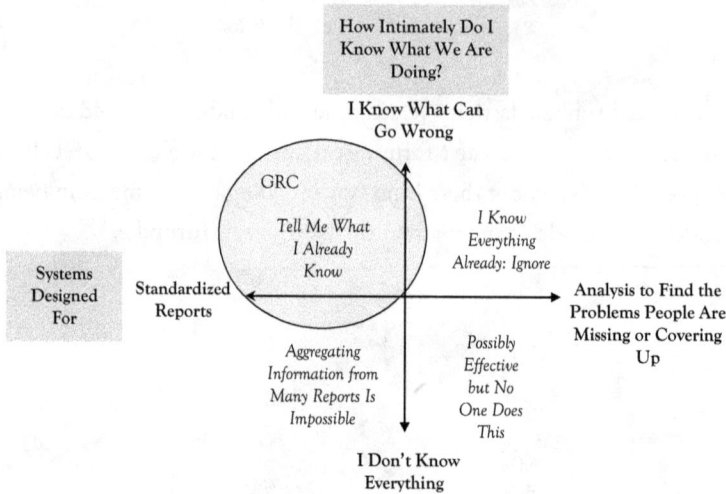

This is the primary problem. GRC systems are designed around what people already know can go wrong, which likely means already has gone wrong. This is like me and my tires. I know you have to put air in them. I know they have a bead—because I had to get that fixed before. I didn't know they could just "dry out."

It was outside my experience. And taking information from outside of one's preexisting set of knowledge is not an easy task. My first reaction was, *Repair shops are a scam. You just want me to buy new tires. I have plenty of tread. I know my rights.* I have seen the same thing happen in meetings where: *I know our employees wouldn't open fake accounts. You're just upset because you haven't been able to sell as many products as your co-workers.* Or, *We don't discriminate, black people just have less money to buy a house.* Fill in your own story here. Feel free to use any examples from the beginning of this book.

Donald Rumsfeld, former U.S. Secretary of Defense, famously said:

Reports that say that something hasn't happened are always interesting to me, because as we know, there are known knowns; there are things we know we know. We also know there are known unknowns; that is to say we know there are some things we do not know. But there are also unknown unknowns—the ones we don't know we don't know. And if one looks throughout the history of our country and other free countries, it is the latter category that tends to be the difficult ones.

Whatever you think about Mr. Rumsfeld's politics and his legacy, he distilled the problem that banking compliance and GRC systems face rather neatly. *But,* you may argue, *I thought you said the problem was fraud and that's not an unknown.* True, but fraud has the evolutionary capability of the COVID virus. Through the application of regulatory fines it morphs and reemerges as, say, cryptocurrency (don't believe me? I've got a chapter on that later). And as regulatory interest wavers, it returns to its previous forms of scam calls and credit card interest rates. In that fluidity of form, how fraud actually occurs day-to-day is an unknown unknown.

To go into a bit more depth, here are some of the key reasons GRC systems are locked in the known–known paradigm. This will get a bit technical, so I will do my best to explain, as I do, with bizarrely chosen analogies.

GRC systems require everyone to conform to one operational paradigm. As we've seen, there are many, many regulations and therefore multiple groups within a company trying to keep track of their rules, policies, procedures, and so on. As a reminder, here's a potential, overlapping, and incomplete list: business continuity, information security, privacy, AML, KYC, lending origination, lending servicing, disclosures, personal account dealing, and so on.

A typical GRC system gets its start in one of these areas, where it may work very well, and then, because that team seems to have its act together, the same system gets pushed into all the other uses—where it was not originally designed to operate. Whatever nuances are needed by the other teams are either ignored or bolted on—leading to either people working outside of the system for data they need or the whole system becoming more complex for everyone.

Here's an analogy, the Swiss Army knife. I have several and I've used the tiny scissors for cutting my fingernails, but I never use it for anything else. It's a terrible: screwdriver, bottle opener, saw, tweezer, drill, corkscrew, ruler, magnifying glass, and pocket light. GRC systems are the same, good at one thing, awful at many, leaving people to go get their own screwdriver or Microsoft Office documents. GRC systems are fertile breeding grounds for off-the-radar SharePoints.

GRC approaches are either bottom up or top down. Closely aligned to the last issue is that GRC systems are designed either for management or for employees. Employees need to be able to, for example, track mortgage applications, make sure all the documentation aligns with the legal requirements, and track complaints and issues. Management needs to know, in aggregate, how the company is doing in all areas of compliance risk.

Fundamentally, the granularity of information needed at the business operational level differs from management. As we talked about earlier, combining risk information cannot be done through an algorithm, people's opinions have to be brought in to weigh the relative risk of selling reverse-mortgages to the elderly versus providing financial management to oligarchs.

A bottom-up GRC system will require significant "bolting on" to allow the subjective risk rating, and conversely a top-level risk assessment system will require complete rewiring to house customer complaint information. Both approaches result in a system conflicted between two use cases and ends up satisfying neither.

GRC systems rely on a single taxonomy. We've discussed taxonomy before and specifically how any given slicing up of the world is going to result in overlap.[1] Up until now, the impossibility of a MECE set of concepts for compliance has been one of endless meetings where people argue if KYC is part of AML or if privacy is part of information security. Meetings are bad enough, but when you try to put these "tags" on data in a system, now we are dealing with garbage to the power of automation.

---

[1] An iconic example from biological taxonomies is the platypus. It lays eggs, has webbed feet, and a bill, but isn't a duck or a bird. It's a mammal. You could pretend Australia doesn't exist, and that's up to you.

In the episode, *Chirp Sorts it Out (Sort of)*, of the TV show, *Peep and The Big Wide World*, a program ostensibly about teaching children colors or the value of friendships, we are instead introduced to some advanced information science concepts. Namely, how MECE fails us in the fuzzily edged world of human concepts. *Plato be damned*, Peep, a yellow bird-slash-circle, does not say, at least not out loud, when he chides his friend Chirp, a red bird, for attempting to apply Platonic orthodoxy to what is clearly a subjective discipline, namely putting stuff into piles.

To wit, Chirp creates piles of blue things, yellow things, shiny things, but what about shiny blue things? A new pile? What about things that look like worms? Wormy green things? The situation escalates as Chirp forcibly places the other characters, the aforementioned yellow Peep and the blue duck(?) Quack who looks more like a bagpipe sans the pipes—even though other ducks look like ducks. Peep is placed with Quack in a "friends" pile and then resorted into "yellow" and "blue" piles—leading Quack to say: *You shouldn't put your friends in piles.* So true.

You think I am making fun? You think I am not serious? I showed this video to several managing directors at a bank and they all agreed that the lessons here were directly applicable to the multihundred, million-dollar GRC project going awry.

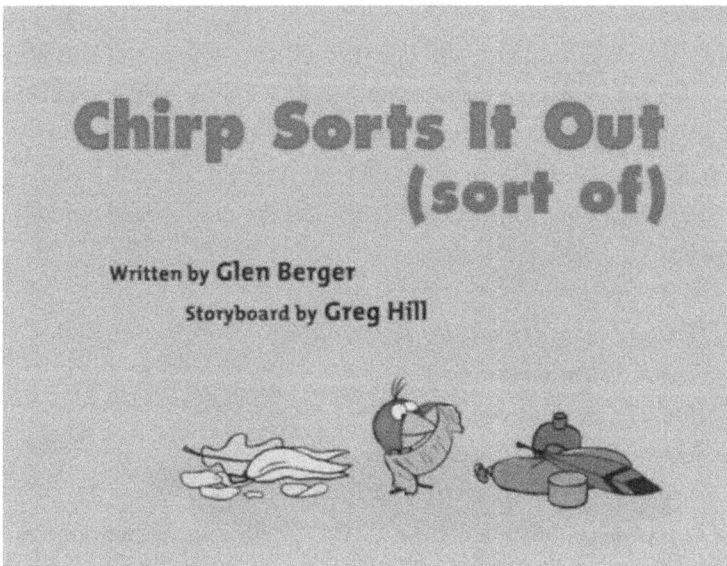

The solution is to allow as many tags as people want on any given data element and not require it to be in one pile. You can have blue things, checkered things, crinkly things, and the sets can overlap, or not, and not everything needs a given tag set, for example, not all items need color tags. Or in compliance, not everything has to be tagged to either being about or not about Regulation Q: Capital Adequacy of Bank Holding Companies, Savings and Loan Holding Companies, and State Member Banks.

Lots of modern computer systems have this kind of flexible tagging approach, Amazon, Twitter, YouTube, Reddit, and so on. Yet somehow in GRC land, the reliance on one taxonomy to rule them all has remained entrenched.

GRC systems focus on tagged data and largely ignore full text. GRC's data structures are much like basic Excel, rows and columns. The rows have individual laws, policy names, issues, and so on. The columns are the data "fields" and are things like date, owner, status, and so on. It is that last field, the one called *description* or *text* where the real valuable information resides. Namely, the text of the law, policy or procedure, the text of customer complaint, the issue description in an, er, issue, the findings in an audit or commentary in a regulatory letter.

The row and column view may be perfectly fine for viewing or entering data (sometimes), but it fails as a data representation for finding things that aren't directly in one of the structured fields or that have not been hand classified a la Chirp with one or more tags. The reason is that the GRC systems have only the most rudimentary full-text search capability, which is hard for them to improve on because of the way the systems are designed and used. The exact reasons are complicated, and I will dive deeper in a bit, but for now, think of it like the drunk searching for his keys under a streetlight.

> *Did you lose your keys under the streetlight?*
> *No, I lost them over there.*
> *Then why are you looking here?*
> *Because this is where the light is.*

Any new system takes time to bring live and to migrate from existing systems. Spend any time in the corporate world and you will find yourself entering data into some cumbersome system that seems like it was created only a few weeks after people stopped using tick marks on whale bones for accounting. Strange selection menus. Screens that don't save unless you click "save." Arcane error messages, "B341: Data type not recognized."

You will be told this will all be fixed when the new system arrives. This will be repeated to you for several years in a row. Then, one magical day, the new system will be turned on. And, you won't have access. A few weeks later they will fix that. And, all of your data will be missing. Or partially missing. Or all there but with data in the wrong fields. And the system will be taken down for maintenance. And so on, around the company and around the world.

Once you are up and running, the workflow turns out to be inflexible and the taxonomy, argued about in all those many meetings still isn't right. Your old cranky system now seems a fond memory, although that's because you missed out on its first decade of life and forget that you managed it by keeping a spreadsheet of your own on the side. No matter, you will be making a SharePoint to keep your data in now and the shiny new system is reduced to being a genuflection to the high priests of the GRC.

Thus, compliance data is largely managed by hand, even though it looks like everyone is using a computer. This is why there are thousands of people in Compliance. To keep track of all the data and to be a human search engine.

Let's explore a bit more what we do know about the unknown unknowns and what I mean by "thousands of people in Compliance" and "human search engine."

How Many People Are in Compliance?

How many people do you need in legal and compliance? Looking at some of the biggest financial institutions, they have about 1 to 3 percent of staff in Legal and Compliance. Of those, about 10 to 30 percent are legal. Of the compliance staff, about 30 to 50 percent are in AML or other transaction monitoring kinds of roles, another 20 to 30 percent are in testing, and the rest are in "general compliance," meaning all the regs that aren't

AML/KYC/BSA.[2] I realize that's a lot of percentages of percentages, so here's an example, very roughly speaking:

Amalgamated Global Bank, Inc.:
250,000 employees total
1,500 Legal
4,000 Compliance
> 1,200 AML/KYC/BSA or other transaction monitoring
> 800 Testing
> 2,000 "other" compliance

As they say, YMMV (your mileage may vary), but this is a pretty good indicator of the kinds of staffing you'll see at a bank that's had any sort of regulatory oversight.

And these people are not cheap. Consider that a Juris Doctor (JD) is equivalent to a PhD in terms of time, but far more expensive. Not everyone in Compliance is a lawyer, but a lot of them are. Typical annual pay ranges are, as of 2022:

Transaction Monitor	$40,000 to $60,000
Junior staff	$60,000 to $120,000
Middle management	$150,000 to $300,000
Senior management	$250,000 to $600,000
Chief Compliance Officer	$250,000 to $1,000,000+

Good work in one sense. Horrible corporate slogging in another. Regardless, the thing to do now is multiply the number of people by the pay to come up with, oh my, $1 to $2 billion or more a year for a major financial company's legal and compliance functions. What are they all doing for that much money?

Back to Fines

They are trying to stop all the fines! I know you knew that. That was in the first chapter, after all. But how do you stop fines? You will be unsurprised

---

[2] Anti-money Laundering, Know Your Customer, Bank Secrecy Act.

that we need some more context and thus I move to a frolic and detour—which is an actual legal term of art, by the by. Here comes the frolic:

On March 29, 2016 a one Abigail Strubel sued Capital One Bank over the disclosures in her credit card agreement. She, and her attorneys, Brian Lewis Bromberg, Jonathan Robert Miller, Bromberg Law Office, P.C., and Harley Jay Schnall, Law Office of Harley J. Schnall, alleged that the font size was too small. Specifically, that the "model forms" offered by the CFPB used 10 point Arial, and that Capital One had used 10 point Garamond LC, which, they argued, was not *clear and conspicuous.*

Amazingly few discotheques provide jukeboxes.	A pangram (all 26 letters) in Arial 10 pts.
Puzzled women bequeath jerks very exotic gifts.	Another pangram in Garamond 10 pts.

Why didn't the bank just use Arial like the CFPB suggested? Did Capital One really try to pull a fast one via leading and kerning? Garamond is noticeably smaller at the same font size. Or did someone just think it looked better with all those nifty serifs everywhere? Did they just hate Arial—I can sympathize, it is everywhere? But perhaps the maxim to never attribute to malice that which is best explained by incompetence applies here.

However the selection of font was made, since it wasn't Arial, now the bank had to instead roll out their own attorneys: Seth A. Schaeffer, Bryan A. Fratkin, McGuireWoods, LLP, Richmond, VA, Jeffrey James Chapman, McGuireWoods LLP, New York, NY, for Defendant.

Ultimately the font didn't matter, it was still legible and the CFPB suggested Arial, but didn't require it. The Court found for the Bank and, in a step one might view as a bit of sass, noted, deep in the 12-page decision: *The Court evaluates the adequacy of TILA disclosures "from the vantage point of a hypothetical average consumer—a consumer who is neither particularly sophisticated nor particularly dense."* A statement so evocative, that it would be cited three years later by a different judge in *Tucker v. Chase Bank U.S.* I feel for Abigail as one might read that sentence and think the judge was saying for someone to be unable to read Garamond typeface, they would have to be unusually unsophisticated or, er, stupid.

As a reminder, and I can't stress this enough, this is all public record. You can look it up whenever you like. And when you do, you may find that this wasn't Abigail's first rodeo with Reg Z.

> *On June 27, 2012, Strubel opened a Victoria's Secret brand credit card account, using the card to purchase a $19.99 article of clothing.1 The credit card agreement provided by Comenity to Strubel disclosed certain consumer rights under amendments to the TILA effected by the Fair Credit Billing Act, Pub. L. No. 93-495, 88 Stat. 1500 (1974).*
>
> *One year later, on June 27, 2013, Strubel filed this putative class action, seeking statutory damages under the TILA for alleged defects in the aforementioned disclosures.*

Unfortunately, Abigail failed to convince the court the earlier occasion as well and whatever relief of her bills she had hoped for was likely overwhelmed by attorney fees. Further, a quick search on casetext.com returns more than 1,000, they stop counting hits at 1,000, of similar attempts arguing small print means someone should not have to pay their bill.

Whatever your view of the relative density of these plaintiffs, they were not fishing in an empty pond. It's just not a lake that regular folks normally get anything out of without the help of the government. Regulators can and do complain about fonts. Here's a sample from April 22, 2022:

> *CFPB Charges TransUnion and Senior Executive John Danaher with Violating Law Enforcement Order*
>
> *For consumers looking for a way out of their subscriptions, TransUnion not only failed to offer a simple mechanism for cancellation, it actively made it arduous for consumers to cancel through clever uses of font and color on its website.*

While the CFPB noted, "*Danaher recently separated from TransUnion,*" I am sure this was still not good news for the company. Whether

Mr. Danaher is there or not, they are going to have to do, as Ricky Ricardo would say, "a lot of 'splainin." It is that "'splainin" that is the real cost for financial companies and it all starts with the same thing you and I dreaded as children: exams.

Regulatory Exams

Stopping fines for a bank means, by and large, passing regulatory exams. An exam is when a regulator shows up either as planned or for a surprise visit and says, "Tell me how you have been complying with Regulation X"—where X is any regulation and not just the CFPB's *Reg X Real Estate Settlement Procedures Act*, nor the *Federal Reserve Board's Reg X Borrowers of Securities Credit*.

These exams are routine, and for any global financial company there may be 20simultaneously going on around the world at any given time. They are so regular an occurrence that some regulators literally maintain a cadre of employees on site at big banks they really want to pay attention to.

And each and every exam runs the risk of causing a fine of thousands, millions, or billions of dollars and a consent order that may, as has happened, put a cap on bank assets or prevent any acquisitions. While Abigail and her compatriots only succeeded at causing banks to spend some money on outside counsel, it is regulatory exams where those hundreds or thousands of compliance staff and the millions or billions of dollars they cost really come into play.

Did you think Compliance departments were there to protect you, the customer? It may be overly cynical, but it could be argued only in as much as it prevents regulators coming down on them.

When an exam starts, a bank will be asked to produce all related materials, which are pretty much the pillars discussed earlier: policies, procedures, regulatory requirements, risk assessments, self-identified issues, audit findings, regulatory findings, and anything else the regulator thinks might be useful.

For an exam about our example of font size we're going to want to look at some regulations. Here they are, fear not!

12 CFR 1015 Mortgage Assistance Relief Services (Reg O)—the CFPB Reg O, not the OCC's Reg O Insider Loans. Capish?

The notice must be made in a clear and prominent manner, on a separate written page, and preceded by heading: "IMPORTANT INFORMATION FROM YOUR [name of lender or servicer] ABOUT THIS OFFER." The heading must be in bold face font that is two-point-type larger than the font size of the required disclosure.

12 CFR 1011 - Purchasers' Revocation Rights, Sales Practices And Standards (Regulation K)—the CFPB again, and not the Fed's Reg K International Banking Operations.

If the advertising is of a classified type; is not more than five inches long and not more than one column in print wide, the disclaimer statement may be set in type of at least six point font.

12 CFR 740 - Accuracy Of Advertising And Notice Of Insured Status

Each insured credit union must also display the official sign on its Internet page, if any, where it accepts deposits or open accounts, but it may vary the font sizes from that depicted in paragraph (b) of this section to ensure its legibility.

12 CFR 1022 - Fair Credit Reporting (Reg V) There's only the one Reg V!

[…]

(vi) Each character of the text required in paragraph (b)(4)(ii) and (v) of this section shall be, at minimum, the same size as the largest character on the page, including characters in an image or graphic banner;

(vii) Each character of the disclosure shall be displayed as plain text and in a sans serif font, such as Arial;

[...]

17 CFR 248.3 Commodities and Securities Regulation S-P: Privacy of Consumer Financial Information and Safeguarding Personal Information

(c)(2)(ii)[...]

(B) Use a typeface and type size that are easy to read;

(C) Provide wide margins and ample line spacing;

(D) Use boldface or italics for key words; and

(E) Use distinctive type size, style, and graphic devices, such as shading or sidebars when you combine your notice with other information.

And many, many more.

Thus the bank will need to find: all of these regulations,[3] the associated policies and procedures, any issues that have been reported about same, any tests, assessments, audits, and, ideally, anything in case law or from other companies—which may come in handy to get a sense of "is this a one off?" or "is there something going on industry-wide." A regulator is always happier when you beg for forgiveness versus trying to argue that what you have been doing, which you might not have even been aware of until now, is, of course, right.

So What Does Compliance Really Do?

How are you going to get all this stuff? There isn't a box labeled "in case of regulatory exam, break glass" on the wall, nor does it contain a folder saying, "everything you always were too disinterested to know about typography and banking, but suddenly have need for now."

You may try to use the intranet first, if you were born yesterday that is. Everyone else knows it's going to give you a million hits, the first one will be the Asia Pacific Marketing Style Guide, which lists the preferred font for investment banking pitch books—probably, ugh, Arial.

You will then, if you know about it and have access, try the GRC system. Chances are near 100 percent that your bank has not classified regulatory obligations by the requirement of typeface. Recall that current GRC systems largely put things into individual buckets, so there's no room for that kind of tagging. And, if by some miracle, the tag does

---

[3] You may have thought that everyone just knew what the law was. Or at least, if the bank doesn't know, then the regulators know. Nope. There's just too many laws and regulations and too many nuances to how they apply based on a given bank's products and services. Figuring out which laws apply is a full-time job. Often many full-time jobs. I once naively asked a Chief Compliance Officer to see the list of all the rules the bank had to comply with. He told me to shut up.

exist, it will almost certainly be out of date—unless this exact same exam happened last month—because why would anyone maintain those tags?

You are going to have to resort to the corporate search engines: phone calls, Outlook, and the company directory. You will search for people in Compliance and start calling them. They will call other people. Who will do what you did, but they will know the systems better and their searches may turn up something useful.

They will have to search for all the variations of words they can think of including: *typeface, type size, point size, small print, fine print, graphic devices, Arial, plain text, sans serif, sans-serif*—depending if the search engine can distinguish with and without a hyphen. But also none of these because as we can see from the regulatory text "*bold face font that is two-point-type larger*" it doesn't say "*font size*" anywhere. And who knows what the policies, procedures, and so on say. Just hope and pray they don't, but probably do say, "employees must follow the requirements of associated regulations."

The process looks like this:

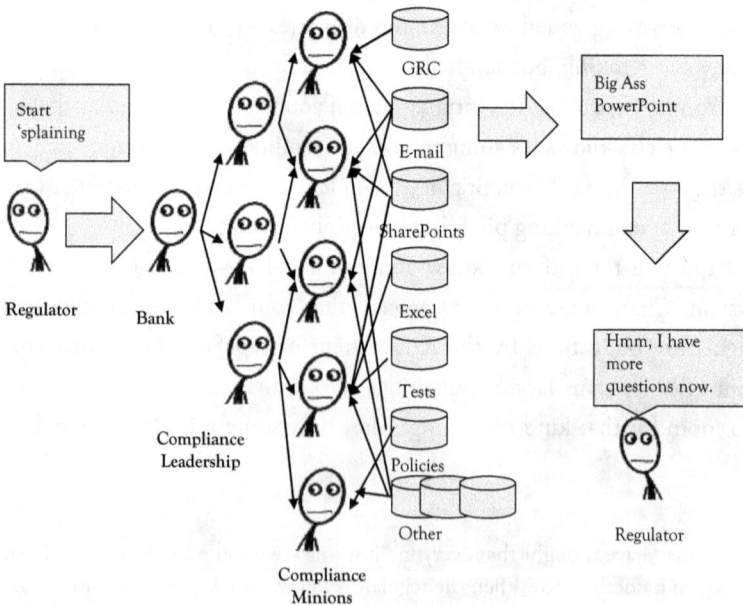

My amazing drawing skills aside, this is obviously oversimplified. In one exam I was part of, the regulator had 20 questions that required more than 50 people directly and over 200 indirectly to look at data from 23 different systems. This, as noted, is happening every day at every large bank.

And when the work's all done, the PowerPoint is filed away, much like the Holy Grail in *Indiana Jones*, except instead of a warehouse of crates, it's in a SharePoint, which is essentially the same in terms of ever locating it again.

What About Artificial Intelligence?

AI/ML stands for Artificial Intelligence/Machine Learning. People think it will solve the problems with, well, everything. Why? Because people love magic.

Don't get me wrong, AI/ML technology can be amazing. Here's a bowl of soup with a monster knitted from wool made by the DALL-E 2 software. That's pretty cool, right?

It also has applications in sorting through millions of transactions to help identify patterns of fraud or money laundering—although the majority of that detection is done with rules rather than just turning an AI model loose on the data.

This is because AI is not like a human brain—mainly because we don't know how human brains work. But also because AI is ultimately just statistical fitting of data. A "learning algorithm" has to be presented with thousands, millions, or billions of data points that are known to be fraud or not to be able to guess if a transaction is or isn't one to flag. This is great for, say, scanning handwritten addressed envelopes to read the character

because there are zillions (technical term) of letters, and their correct text, available as data.

Where AI fails is on anything outside of the existing data. That's why it can play chess but not predict the stock market. And for AML and other monitoring at banks, rules have been the solution far more than AI.

There's much better explanations out there, but the main point is AI is more marketing than substance when it comes to being better at locating and managing compliance information. The *New York Times* put it better than I can when they took on the clay feet of IBM's Watson AI:

> *IBM started with cancer. It sought out medical centers where research-ers worked with huge troves of data. The idea was that Watson would mine and make sense of all that medical information to improve treatment.*
>
> *At the University of North Carolina School of Medicine, one of IBM's partners, the difficulties soon became apparent. The oncolo-gists, having seen Watson's "Jeopardy!" performance, assumed it was*

an answer machine. The IBM technologists were frustrated by the complexity, messiness and gaps in the genetic data at the cancer center.

"We thought it would be easy, but it turned out to be really, really hard," said Dr. Norman Sharpless, former head of the school's cancer center, who is now the director of the National Cancer Institute.

[...]

IBM discontinued Watson for Genomics, which grew out of the joint research with the University of North Carolina. It also shelved another cancer offering, Watson for Oncology, developed with another early collaborator, the Memorial Sloan Kettering Cancer Center.

In the meantime, I want to move forward about the real problem with compliance, which isn't about technology. And, I suspect, why I didn't hear back from that general counsel. Let's get to the heart of the matter...

CHAPTER 5

Why Does Financial Crime Keep Happening?

We've talked about the enormous fines, we've looked at the armies of compliance people, and yet, as a quick Internet search will testify, it keeps on keeping on. Why? Why don't financial professionals just stop? Why don't Compliance people stop them?

When I first started writing this book, I considered that it could be as simple as this: a nice hardbound spine with a title of *Why Don't Banks Comply with the Law?*, a single sentence on page 1: *Because they don't want to.* And then, a few hundred blank pages so you at least got something for your money.

Maybe that's the book I should have written. It's not untrue. Yet, as we've seen, banks do spend a lot on Compliance and there are many people employed with Compliance as their career. Is it all a sham? Essentially yes, but let's not be quick to blame well-meaning people both on the business and Compliance sides.

There are serious, and not so serious, attempts to make things right, so let's look at the potential solutions proffered by various parties and see where they each fall short. The fixes we will examine are as follows:

Compliance Departments at big banks
Financial and FinTech start-ups
Crypto Finance
Regulators

Each has been offered up to stop the abuses of finance, by hand, through technology, and through wholesale rethinking of how finance works.

Compliance Departments at Big Banks
Aka Three Lines of Defense

I was once at a meeting with a regulator and they said to the CCO seated next to me:

When will you stop harming customers?[1]

There was, understandably, a pregnant pause. This may sound like the old loaded question, *Have you stopped beating your wife?* But since we were there to talk about the multiple consent orders against the bank, some of which had been going on for years, it wasn't so much loaded as exasperated.

The CCO gamely started walking through the several dozen project plans underway to address the failures the regulators had identified. It was a good try and that CCO lasted almost a full year longer in the job.

I'm not trying to be funny. Turnover of senior staff is a key tactic from banks when dealing with compliance problems. At one bank I saw five CCOs in four years. At another it was three in three years. That is not uncommon.

Moving further down the management chain to division and corporate senior compliance staff, I have seen nearly complete rollover of staff two or three times over the same period. One project I worked on I kept a list of all the people replaced on the project, and when it was around 100 I put my name on the list. It was all *that bad apple's fault*. Remember when we talked about bad apples back in the beginning of the book? We've finally come to why it's not about bad apples.

Three Lines of Defense Don't Work

Compliance at large banks follows the "three lines of defense" model. I mentioned this before in passing, so it bears a little more explanation. The business itself is called the *first line of defense*. Functional areas such as Compliance, HR, Technology are known as the second line. And Audit is the third line. Further, Audit itself has both an internal team of auditors and an external audit firm. So maybe think of those as lines 3A and 3B.

Each line is supposed to be independent. The first line checks itself through a "Control" group, the second line checks the first, and Audit

---

[1] Hey, that's the title of the book!

checks the first and second. Then, because Audit reports to the Audit Committee of the Board, it can route around the chain of command to stop bad behavior.

This is a high-level view, and each bank implements it in their own unique way—often changing the approach and specific roles and responsibilities annually. I have sat in many meetings where we had no mini-bagels, but lots of PowerPoint slides and expensive consultants going line by line through who is where on a "RACI" diagram.

RACI stands for responsible, accountable, consulted, or informed, and so the question is posed, "Is Compliance responsible for knowing the law?" Or is it Legal? Or the business? Or is the business "accountable for the law"? Or is the business "consulted" about the law or "informed"? What about regulatory policies? Procedures? Controls? Training? What about Audit? What are they "responsible" for?

Unsurprisingly, these meetings spin for hours often with a lot of time being spent retrading what "responsible," "accountable," "consulted," and "informed" mean much less who ends up with which term for which pillar.

The Europeans claim to have invented the three lines of defense in 2008, to quote the Internet: *The Three Lines of Defense Model was developed in 2008–10 by the Federation of European Risk Management Associations (FERMA) and the European Confederation of Institutes of Internal Auditing (ECIIA) as a guidance for the 8th EU Directive Art. 41 2b.* However, I have seen it in practice since at least 2004, and it almost certainly goes back long before then.

It doesn't work. One way to tell it has failed is all of the fines, and especially repeat fines and consent orders for failures of compliance at all the biggest banks. I was thinking I would name a few here, but it is literally all of them. There is not a bank that is a household name that isn't also subject to repeat regulatory action over the course of decades. Here's an excellent summary of the top 10 from the excellent *Good Jobs First* website that was also the source of some of the data way back in the introduction.

The continued failures should be enough to throw out the three lines on evidence alone. The cause should also be self-evident, the first line is in charge. The second and third line can complain all they want. You can

Financial Firm	Fines since 2000	Number of Regulatory Records
Bank of America	$82,898,016,192	264
JPMorgan Chase	$36,127,193,625	218
Citigroup	$25,540,645,217	156
Wells Fargo	$21,881,892,841	222
Deutsche Bank	$18,341,457,302	76
UBS	$16,879,318,334	102
Goldman Sachs	$16,399,485,793	87
NatWest Group PLC	$13,515,546,857	31
BNP Paribas	$12,148,363,950	19
Credit Suisse	$10,732,400,126	49

hire the best and brightest and most sincere Compliance staff. Ultimate decision making remains with the foxes running the hen house.

As soon as the consent orders are lifted, banks go back to their previous behavior, until they get another consent order. I liken it to a dental patient getting a root canal. The compliance team is leaning over the businesses open mouth, which is full of tubes and implements, when the regulator walks in the room and says, "looking good!," at which point the business jumps up from the chair, pulls off the little blue bib, and starts to stride out of the room, tubes in tow. *But we aren't done!* Compliance protests. *You heard the man, good enough!* Says the business, fading into the distance.

Let's take an example, new products. A new product (or service) offering developed by a business needs to go through a thorough "New Product Review." Compliance and Legal typically have to provide sign off as part of the process. And at every bank I know of, either having worked there or known people there, the New Product Review policy and process are a first priority of regulators, especially following an enforcement action.

The new policy is carefully crafted, edited by management, approved at a Board meeting, and combed through by Audit before showing it to the regulators who also examine the new policy, the process, the shiny new computer application, and look through a few months of reports. Great. Good. Solved! Done. Dusted. Everyone moves on.

But there's a little carve out. Nothing big. Not to worry. Hey, it's just a footnote if it's mentioned at all—it's so obvious. If your product is just a modification of an existing one, then it's not "new." It doesn't have to go through all the layers and steps. And goodness knows, the complexity has gone up an order of magnitude in direct response to the regulatory scrutiny. And so we don't want to burden the business with having to submit a full review if it's just a tweak. That would hurt competitiveness.

I will let you guess who decides if it is a new product or a revised product. I will also let you guess the amount of paperwork required for a revision. And finally, suppose how many products are "new" versus "revisions." If you said, the business decides if it is new or not, there's no compliance paperwork for revised products, and most products are revisions, give yourself a high five and take the afternoon off. You have just routed around ~~the controls in place to stop abuse in the wake of fines~~, corporate red tape.

And what happens to Compliance and Audit staff when they raise their voices about these end runs? That's what's known as a career limiting move. And then we get the bad apples. And the new crop of apples coming in, from another bank—where they were the bad apples there—but are now going to solve all the problems, until they too, ultimately, get blamed. I just hope, for their sake, they get their stock options at least.

Financial and FinTech Start-Ups

Start-ups in finance are all about trying to make the world a better place. Or at least, that's what their marketing literature says. My search for "fin tech save the world" returned 39,600,000 results. That's a lot of world saving. Promises include: stopping climate change, banking for migrants, effortless international money transfers, mortgages for everyone, an end to poverty. Just imagine if any of it worked!

What you won't see is how they will improve compliance with the law. For many, especially crypto finance, it is specifically how they will eliminate the need for regulation. No law equals nothing to have to comply with. We will get to that more later.

Google   fintech save the world   ✕   Q

Q All   🗏 News   🖾 Images   ▶ Videos   🛒 Shopping   ⋮ More   Tools

About 39,600,000 results (0.30 seconds)

https://www.fundthrough.com › FundThrough Blog   ⋮
Top 3 Ways Fintech Is Saving the World - FundThrough
From mobile banking to radically changing how we transfer money abroad, Fintech is making
the world a better place. See how you can join the movement.

https://www.businessandindustry.co.uk › Fintech   ⋮
How fintech is saving the planet - Business & Industry
Nov 16, 2021 — Bringing technology and finance together unlocks the system-change needed to
save the planet. This is a huge opportunity and responsibility ...

https://ffnews.com › thought-leader › how-fintech-can-...   ⋮
How Fintech can help people save the planet
Oct 12, 2020 — One of the largest crises our humanity will ever face is global warming and
climate change. Can fintech help us to face this global crisis?

https://podcasts.apple.com › podcast › episode-416-can... ○ ⊕   ⋮
Episode 416: Can Fintech Save the Planet? Breaking Banks

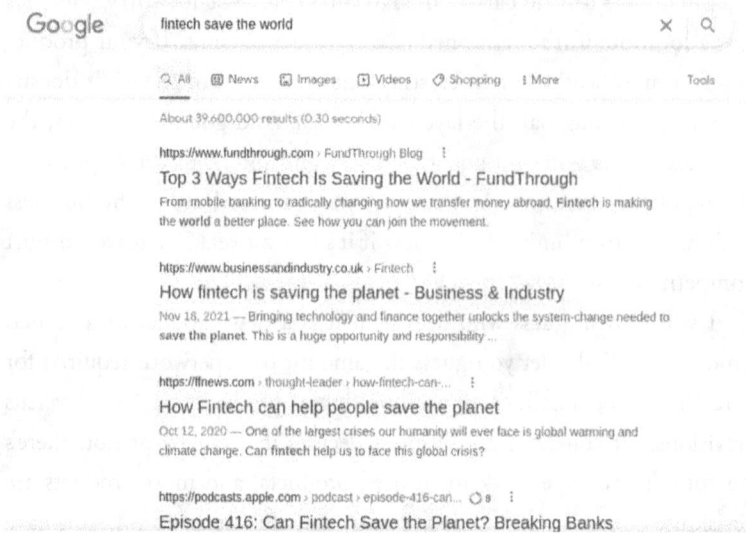

What I want to address here is that financial start-ups are just that, start-ups, and therefore have more limited resources than Amalgamated Universal. Here's a fictional head of compliance job posting that I compiled from actual want ads I regularly see:

> *Head of Compliance, responsibilities include: BSA/AML money laundering officer, handles compliance with privacy, broker dealer, fiduciary, payments, consumer protection and all banking letter regulations, write compliance policies and procedures, monitor changes in regulations in US, US states, Canada and its provinces, UK, and Asia, meet with regulators, meet with clients, meet with investors, train staff, must have series 7, 63, 66, 65, 24. Team will initially consist of just the Head of Compliance. 15+ years relevant experience and JD preferred.*
>
> *Salary: ½ to ⅓ of equivalent at large bank*

Recall when I said that big banks have 1 to 3 percent of staff allocated for Legal and Compliance? If you carry that to the logical extreme for a 100-person start-up, that's 1 to 3 compliance people. But that logic doesn't work. Like doctors, Compliance people are specialists. Here's an anecdote you didn't ask for:

I was visiting friends and laying on their floor. I was horizontal because I had severe vertigo. The room spun like a camera wielded by a toddler. Luckily my friend was a neurosurgeon.

His wife asked, *Can you help?*
Is he bleeding out of his ears? He asked.
Checked my ears. *No.*
"Then I'm out of ideas."

A neurosurgeon is not a neurologist. And neither of them are radiologists. In the same vein, a web developer isn't a network engineer and neither of them are hardware designers. Or rather, if you find someone who knows about all these things, you've got breadth without depth and vice versa.

FinTech and start-ups literally cannot afford enough compliance staff to know all the areas that they are required to understand. All they can manage is one jack-of-all-trades who they will pay far less than the same person, if qualified, could earn at a big bank.

But FinTech's and start-ups attract the best and brightest? That is true in technology where there's a chance to strike it rich and the ever-changing nature of tech means that hiring someone with only a few years of experience is possible and maybe better. In medicine, you need years of experience with real patients to be able to understand real risks. Legal and compliance are no different. In short, look to innovation as the gateway to the ghost of financial fraud of the past, and, just like big banks, only when they are fined will the compliance staff be enhanced.

June 30, 2021

- *FINRA said it fined Robinhood[2] $57 million and ordered the stock trading app to pay nearly $13 million in restitution to thousands of clients.*

---

[2] You may be thinking that Robinhood got fined because they stoked memes about GameStop stock or that they blocked traders from profiting from those memes. Nope. They got fined because they were terrible at being a trading platform. The confused customers with bad data—so bad that one person committed suicide thinking he owed millions when he did not—they failed to check that people were sophisticated enough to trade options, and their computer systems were unreliable and subject to failure (business continuity!).

- *"Robinhood has invested heavily in improving platform stability, enhancing our educational resources, and building out our customer support and legal and compliance teams," Robinhood said in response to the fine.*

These investments in Compliance will, naturally, mirror the approach at the big banks. Compliance costs money both in terms of people and in limiting the kinds of business that can be done. The sooner we can put these bad apples to rest, the sooner we can get back to pairing down the Compliance team. Or maybe we don't need Compliance at all? Onto Crypto!

Crypto Finance

Can cryptocurrency, decentralized finance, blockchains, non-fungible tokens (NFTs), stablecoins, and so on stop financial crime?

Oh no. God no. Let me, oh, my, let me catch my breath. Just give me a minute. OK, all better. And if that makes sense to you, feel free to skip ahead. You and I are all good. If not, hold on, we're going to have to do this thing.

Let's recall why someone would think crypto might be an improvement. (If any of the following terms are unfamiliar, such as proof-of-work, it is, I'm afraid, beyond the scope of this book, meaning I don't want to explain and you can find many people willing to do so on the Internet. I suggest searching for David Gerard and any concept you'd like expounded upon in a curmudgeonly manner.)

No central authority and trustless. Crypto removes the controlling power of banks and puts it in the hands of the individual investors. Further, you don't need to trust counterparties because the nature of proof-of-work or proof-of-stake transaction management means that no one actor can abuse the system (unless they have more than 51 percent of the compute power or currency, respectively).

Code is law. You can inspect the software that drives a given offering, aka smart contract, and be sure there's no funny business, that is, the disclosure is the source code.

Transactions are public and immutable. If everything is in the open, bad actors can't hide and therefore can't swindle you.

Crypto is open to all. It is the ultimate democracy because everyone is equal online and with anonymous user names no one knows if you are black, white, or purple, and therefore there can be no discriminatory practices.

Easier international transactions. Without the overhead of traditional finance middlemen, payments can happen faster and cross-border payments especially will be near instantaneous.

No need for regulation. All of these factors mean crypto is a truly free market and customers will therefore have perfect information to choose products and services that don't harm them.

These aren't the ideas of madmen. Several people I know and respect personally have espoused them to me—they are true believers who have extensive professional backgrounds in technology, law, or compliance. It isn't these ideas, which are well-intentioned, that are wrong. And it isn't wrong to say traditional finance and associated law isn't working so great—that's a central thesis of this book after all.

However, none of them stand up in the real world. But before we get too deep into the specifics, to give you a flavor of where I will be going, here's the July 2022 crypto edition, with many thanks to Molly White of *web3isgoinggreat.com* for regularly updated postings on the crypto space.

July 1, 2022	Quixotic NFT marketplace hacked for $100,000.
July 4, 2022	CoinLoan *temporary restriction applies to the total amount of daily withdrawals per account: every user can withdraw up to $5,000 per 24-hour rolling period.* Down from $500,000 per day.
July 5, 2022	Voyager digital files for bankruptcy. Creditors will likely wait months to years to get their money, if at all. One of the letters to the bankruptcy court written by a customer states: *I log into my Voyager account; it reads "You own XX.X Bitcoin (BTC)." However, we read the notes from the first day hearing; and the lawyers representing Voyager state in your court that the cryptocurrency*

that the customers bought was never theirs and it is all Voyager's property. I hope Voyager does not get to walk away with our hard-earned assets.

July 6, 2022   Genesis Capital has losses due to earlier failure of counterparty 3AC. Internet chatter puts the number at "hundreds of millions of dollars."

July 6, 2022   South Korea's Uprise reportedly loses $20 million of customer funds by betting that the Luna crypto token would go down. Luna did collapse, but not before a short squeeze—brief rises in the price—wiped out Uprise on margin calls.

July 7, 2022   Spanish cryptocurrency platform 2gether was *forced to close service for private accounts* due to *lack of resources and crypto winter.*

July 8, 2022   Hypernet Labs shuts down. Founder tweets: *Unfortunately, the treasury was also held in Ethereum, which disproportionately exacerbated the bear market's impact on our balance sheet.* Coincidentally, a $1 million lawsuit was recently filed against Hypernet in New Zealand alleging fraud.

July 8, 2022   News breaks that Blockchain.com has told shareholders that they stand to lose $270 million from 3AC bankruptcy. Everyone was a counterparty to 3AC.

July 8, 2022   Vauld files for protection from creditors, equivalent to U.S. bankruptcy. Reports allege over $400 million owed to creditors.

July 10, 2022   Hacker steals $2.25 million from Bifrost platform.

July 10, 2022   Hacker steals $1.43 million from Omni NFT platform.

July 11, 2022   Hacker steals $100,000 from Citizen Finance.

July 11, 2022   Hacker steals $8.17 from Uniswap platform.

July 13, 2022   Crypto lender Celsius files for bankruptcy. Filings indicate that Celsius owes $4.7 billion to its customers and has a hole of $1.2 billion between assets and liabilities.

July 15, 2022* *Federal Court Orders Texas Man [Jimmy Gale Watson, et al.] to Pay Over $290,000 for Manipulative and Deceptive Digital Asset Pump-and-Dump Scheme.* The et al. here is John McAfee of antivirus and bat-shit crazy old man fame. The SEC action lets McAfee officially off the hook for being dead.

July 16, 2022   Hacker steals $150,000 from NFT phishing attack by impersonating artist DeeKay.

July 18, 2022   *The FBI is warning financial institutions and investors about cyber criminals creating fraudulent cryptocurrency investment applications (apps) to defraud cryptocurrency investors. [...] The FBI has identified 244 victims and estimates the approximate loss associated with this activity to be $42.7 million.*

July 18, 2022   *Supervisor De Nederlandsche Bank (DNB) has imposed a fine of EUR 3.32 million on Binance, the world's largest trading platform for cryptocurrencies. The company has been active in the Netherlands for quite some time without registration, although this is mandatory.* [Google translated from Dutch]

July 18, 2022   Bexplus exchange shuts down. Gives customers 24 hours to withdraw their funds. *We regret to inform you that due to force majeure, Bexplus will stop service from now on.*

July 18, 2022   AEX exchange suspends operation in cooperation with Chinese police inquiry.

July 19, 2022   Hacker steals $20 million from Raccoon Network and Freedom Protocol. Or maybe the founders are the hackers. We'll never know. *PeckShield has detected @RACNETWORK and @freedomprot are scam. [...] Scammers already transferred ~20m $BUSD (IDO) to 0xf800...469336.* Yes, we'll never know. July 17, 2022 Hacker steals PREMINT NFTs. Losses potentially around $300,000.

July 20, 2022   Zipmex stops customer withdrawals. The Thai Securities and Exchange Commission says: ทั้งนี้เนื่องจาก

ข้อมูลที่ได้รับยังขาดสาระสำคัญประกอบการพิจารณาก.ล.ต. จึงมีหนังสือให้ Zipmex ชีแจงรายละเอียดของเหตุการณ์อย่างครบถ้วน. Which Google tells me means: *Due to the lack of material information received for consideration, the SEC has sent a letter to Zipmex to clarify the details of the event in its entirety.*

July 20, 2022   *A team of investigators from the Seoul Southern District Prosecutors Office began seizing transaction records and other materials from Upbit, Bithumb, Coinone, and four other local exchanges.* This is tied to the collapse of Terra Luna platform earlier this year.

July 21, 2022*   *SEC Charges Former Coinbase Manager, Two Others in Crypto Asset Insider Trading Action. "In nearly a year, the defendants collectively earned over $1.1 million in illegal profits by engaging in an alleged insider trading scheme that repeatedly used material, nonpublic information to trade ahead of Coinbase listing announcements."*

July 23, 2022   Hacker steals $1.1 million from Audius.

July 25, 2022   Spice DAO aka Dune DAO folds going from an all-time high of almost $0.002 to $0. Wait, it was already at $0.

July 25, 2022*   *CEO of Titanium Blockchain (TBIS) Pleads Guilty in $21 Million Cryptocurrency Fraud Scheme. Stollery further admitted that he did not use the invested money as promised but instead commingled the ICO investors' funds with his personal funds, using at least a portion of the offering proceeds for expenses unrelated to TBIS, such as credit card payments and the payment of bills for Stollery's Hawaii condominium.*

July 25, 2022   Hacker steals $4.5 million from Teddy Doge. Hackers may be the founders. We will never know. *Wallets connected to Teddy Doge's deployer contract exchanged TEDDY tokens for thousands of wrapped BNB, a BNB equivalent issued on Ethereum, from several accounts over the weekend, security firm PeckShield said on Monday.* We will never know.

July 26, 2022   *The New York Times* reports the Treasury Department is investigating Kraken exchange for violating sanctions.

July 28, 2022   *FDIC and Federal Reserve Board issue letter demanding Voyager Digital cease and desist from making false or misleading representations of deposit insurance status.* You will note this is 20 days after Voyager filed for bankruptcy, but better late than never someone will probably not say.

July 28, 2022   Nirvana finance hacked for $3.5 million.

July 29, 2022   CoinFLEX *had to let go of a significant number of the CoinFLEX team across all departments and geographies. The staff cuts and nonstaff costs that we have made will reduce our cost base by approximately 50–60 percent.* In late June they had stopped withdrawals.

July 29, 2022   *According to a restructuring plan viewed by Bloomberg, Babel's prop desk lost around 8,000 BTC and 56,000 ETH, valued at around $225 million at the time of the loss.* In mid-June Babel had stopped withdrawals.

July 29, 2022   *Web3 darling Helium has bragged about Lime being a client for years. Lime says it isn't true.* Helium also claimed Salesforce as a customer. Also not true.

July 30, 2022   *At least 101 NFT Discords were compromised in July through social engineering collab, audit, bookmark, and impersonation scams* according to OKHotshot on Twitter.

And I know it's outside the cutoff, but we have some good ones from August 1. Please forgive the one day extra.

August 1, 2022   *SEC Charges Eleven Individuals in $300 Million Crypto Pyramid Scheme. Alleged Fraudulent Blockchain Scheme Spanned Multiple Countries Including U.S., Russia.* With this quote: *"Fraudsters cannot circumvent the federal securities laws by focusing their schemes on smart contracts and blockchains."*

August 1, 2022   *Two Orange County Men Sentenced to Federal Prison for Conning Investors Out of $1.9 Million Through Cryptocurrency Offering.*

August 1, 2022   Hackers steal $190 million from Nomad Bridge. *Four days before the attack, Nomad announced that they'd raised a $22.4 million seed round from investors including Coinbase, OpenSea, and Crypto.com.*

* indicates items repeated from earlier July 2022 in the broader financial market. I have attempted to add some added flavor to these to keep them interesting.

On top of all this, here's a quote from a research paper entitled *An Anatomy of Crypto-Enabled Cybercrime.*

BitCoin Abuse registers on average 5,000 cybercrime reports a month. [...] Ransomware dominates cybercrime-related bitcoin activity with 86.7 percent of the total BTC payments.

That was quite a long list. Admittedly less fine-heavy than "trad fi," but impressive nonetheless for the scope. I think we are now ready to revisit those promises of how crypto is better:

No central authority and trustless. Without central authority and no trust in any counterparty there is no one to appeal to when things go wrong. People might not want to have to trust, but they do want the ability to sue. Additionally, in actual practice both proof-of-work and proof-of-stake end up being centralized by a handful of powerful "whales" who can dictate activity.

For example, when the original DAO blew up, the Ethereum foundation unilaterally decided to "hard fork" the protocol. The same happened with Bitcoin. The result is that in crypto you are either a small player, with no recourse, or a big player, who can dictate more than any traditional financial firm. This is like the problem we discussed earlier where the law bends to those with money. In crypto the needle is pegged firmly in the whale's favor, no high-priced lawyers needed.

Code is law. Products on the blockchain are called "smart contracts"—which are really just programs that perform the tasks of old-world concepts such as derivatives, swaps, loans, and so on. The term "smart contract" is not by accident however. The idea is that we replace the fallible and influenceable human concept of courts and judges within an algorithmic construct that is deterministic and incorruptible.

But no one writes perfect code. It may or may not be mathematically possible to write error-free code, but in the real world, bugs are every day. Here's just one example, on September 2, 2022 a company Tweeted this:

> *An exploit was shared with us 30 minutes before mint went live. After reviewing it with 3 different dev teams, we did not believe the credibility of the information sent to us... We were clearly wrong, and we are truly truly sorry.*

This, in itself, is fairly run of the mill, but in this case the firm was Rug Pull Finder, a firm dedicated to finding hacks in other projects and doing code security audits. If they can't get it correct, who can? No one.

When someone gets all their funds stolen through, for example, a common bug in Ethereum contracts that allows repeated siphoning of funds—a "reentrant attack"—there's one view that this is simply the code functioning as implemented, if not as intended. From this vantage point, there is no recourse for the victims. Someone figured out what it *really* did and code is, by fundamental ethic of crypto, the law.

Transactions are public and immutable. The blockchain is purpose built to be immutable. *The moving finger writes; and having writ, moves on: nor all your piety nor wit shall lure it back to cancel half a line, nor all your tears wash out a word of it.* It is unlikely Omar Khayyam was speaking of Bitcoin in the 11th century, but it does correctly describe blockchain—except it doesn't. As noted previously, when there's a big enough theft there will be a desire to wind back the clock, as with the hard forks.

Because of the previous point about all code being subject to unintended error, there's a practical need to be able to modify code on the blockchain without having to go to the extreme of burning all of an existing currency and replacing it fully with newly minted coins.

Smart contracts, which started life as immutable, are now all written in a mutable way. The core operational logic is moved off the blockchain and onto a regular old server. This allows for errors to be fixed, but it also means that customers can't rely on the promise that the code will be publicly available—the private server is, well, private—nor unchanging. There's even open source methods to do this, such as OpenZeppelin—and I don't mean to be too fuddy duddy, but zeppelin? The history of the word is not exactly one swathed in glory.

Further, operating code or storing data on the blockchain can be slow and costly. It's much cheaper, and more reliable pricewise, to operate high-volume transactions and store large files, such as NFT images on Amazon's cloud than the Interplanetary File Server—that's what they call it, and I believe it is only on this one planet for now. All of the real action therefore ultimately happens "off chain" where it is outside of the open transparency promised and immutable only when someone with enough power wants it to be such.

Crypto is open to all. Technology-based revolutions require access to technology. The phrase bandied about crypto is "banking the unbanked." This, of course, requires access to electricity and computers. Estimates on electricity and smartphones show pretty good coverage, about 90 percent and 80 percent, which is impressive. So all good on crypto having a shot at improving banking access.

In the United States, the Government Accounting Office (GAO) estimates that more than 7 million households don't have a bank account, or about 5 percent of the population. The GAO then goes on to indicate how the U.S. government is working to improve financial literacy and increase access to bank accounts. Good news for both traditional and crypto finance, right?

We've made an assumption that everyone needs to have banking in their lives. The GAO summarizes why people don't use banks:

Consumers cited several reasons why they did not have a bank account. Among the top 3 reasons, consumers said that not having enough money, high or unpredictable fees, and distrust of banks were reasons they didn't have accounts. Other reasons cited by consumers included privacy concerns, not qualifying for an account, banks not

*offering the needed services, and the inconvenience of bank hours
and locations.*

These seem like pretty good reasons to me, and likely shared by those
around the world without banking. It certainly doesn't seem like they
would need to be purchasing pictures of digital monkeys—or actually a
string of numbers that links to digital pictures. Nor do they necessarily
want exchange of cash to come with transaction fees—crypto is no different than a credit card, every movement of money takes a fee. We can
debate how big that fee is, it's still more than giving someone a stack of
paper fiat.

Attempts to provide crypto to the masses have only been tried a few
times, most notably in El Salvador where everyone was given a Chivo
crypto wallet in 2022 as government authorized Bitcoin as legal tender. It
did not go well. There was rampant identity theft of the initial $30 given
to all citizens, the network was unstable, transaction fees were all over
the place, fears of being monitored and tracked by the government were
not allayed.

And for the purposes of this book, banking the unbanked is not going
to decrease their risk of being subject to financial frauds. If you don't have
a bank account then bank compliance, by definition, is working just fine
for you!

Easier international transactions. The use case for the unbanked,
and for the less wealthy, that has been espoused is easier transaction, especially cross border. There are a lot of payments made around the world:
Philippine nurses in America or Indian construction workers in the Middle East and anywhere, the poor have traveled to get a paycheck to be able
to send money home. This is a real problem. The costs at Western Union
and other money transmitters are high with intermediaries skimming
from those least able to afford it.

There is undoubtedly a need for better remit methods for small
amounts of money. But the main reason international payments are hard
is money laundering. When funds leave one jurisdiction and travel to
another it can be to avoid taxation or other law enforcement surveillance,
and it's not easy to tell the difference between a farm worker sending a
thousand dollars to the family versus a drug gang mule sending cash from

the sale of heroin or hundreds of small deposits masking the movement of stolen funds to purchase a yacht in Malta. Cash is cash is cash.

In response governments, especially the United States, have imposed ever more restrictions on cross-border money transfers. There are detailed KYC requirements for people to prove they are who they say they are, there is required reporting of large transfers and suspicious-looking transfers of small amounts, and, critically, there are crackdowns on financial institutions if they don't do this. Banks are, whether they want to be or not, effectively law enforcement. Let's recall that the gangster Al Capone was not taken down for murders on St. Valentine's day, but for tax evasion. The government will get their money.

Is this a good system? No. It's cumbersome, costly, slow, and complex. It's a drain on the world and a penalty paid by everyone regardless of your relation to criminal activity. But crypto is not a solution. Crypto attempts to route around AML requirements through technology. It is an escalation of the criminal's capabilities to avoid the system, not a fundamental rethink of how to deal with crime where it occurs, or what crime is in the first place. (Capone existed because of Prohibition, but again, beyond my scope to start talking about the War on Drugs!)

In August 2022, the U.S. Department of the Treasury forced the crypto mixing service Tornado Cash to effectively shut down. A mixer operates by taking a set of transactions, splitting them up into little tiny pieces and shuffling them into a new set of transactions. This circumvents the capability to track who paid whom, which had previously been a core feature. And while the mixing process can sometimes be rewound through diligent analysis, it still serves exactly the same purpose as "layering and integration" in traditional money laundering.

The Feds do not like this anymore than when a regular bank does it. Sanctions violations were the reason behind the biggest single fine in history, BNP Paribas' $8.9 billion penalty in 2014.

Today, Treasury is sanctioning Tornado Cash, a virtual currency mixer that launders the proceeds of cybercrimes, including those committed against victims in the United States," said Under Secretary of the Treasury for Terrorism and Financial Intelligence Brian E. Nelson. "Despite public assurances otherwise, Tornado Cash has repeatedly

failed to impose effective controls designed to stop it from launder-
ing funds for malicious cyber actors on a regular basis and without
basic measures to address its risks. Treasury will continue to aggres-
sively pursue actions against mixers that launder virtual currency for
criminals and those who assist them.

No need for regulation. Crypto is the ultimate in laissez-faire. In one sense, crypto is the 1920s stock market. A free for all of speculation where some win big, many are rendered destitute, celebrities are recruited to provide a patina of allure, for example. Groucho Marx or Larry David, and government is kept well away through "donations" and individual politicians' own dreams of hitting it big.

It was partially this speculation that triggered many bank failures and the Great Depression. This brought the government heavily into financial regulation to create institutions like the FDIC to protect the bank accounts of average depositors. Because the alternative was rampant bank runs where everyone became a loser. We can see shades of this in the abovementioned list of failures in the crypto market and people who thought they were *depositors* discovering that they were actually *investors* and not protected by the FDIC (see the note earlier from July 28 where the FDIC told Voyager to stop saying that they had deposit insurance, after Voyager went bankrupt).

In another sense, crypto is a market whose use case *is* the avoidance of regulation, specifically money laundering. Its primary users viewed either hopefully as political dissidents and refugees or, more cynically, and provably more likely, to be drug cartels, pariah nation states, and financial criminals.

In my view, the promise of crypto is an admirable one: Defeat the worst excesses of crony capitalism through technology and collective ownership. While it technically came from the hard right Austrian school of economics and aligns with gold bug metals-in-my-mattress types, it also shares a lot of ground with communism, collective bargaining, and utopian enclaves of the past like the Amana colony. But when this kind of idealism meets the externalities of normal life it rarely results in a manufacturer of quality refrigerators.

Instead, like actual communism, unions, and utopias, they are almost always corrupted by those who prey on the dreamers. What they do not accomplish is a safer, more functional legal and financial system for the masses. And so no, crypto will not fix or reduce the crime that comes with finance.

Oh and, crypto firms also tend to suffer from the same approach as other financial start-ups, namely one person Compliance departments staffed by people who are willing to claim they know all the regulations, so yeah.

Regulators

Regulators are, like the rest of us, political animals. They have bosses in Washington DC, Sacramento, Albany, and other state capitals you only remember if you ever had a hot dog there. I had a hot dog in Chicago, it had pickles on it and it was delicious. I don't know how regulators feel about sausages, but in terms of putting companies through the grinder, they like to go after crimes that have a big impact on lots of voters or cause harm to the tax coffers. These are the two primary interests of their political leadership.

This could be explored in more depth and a discussion had about the blind eye turned to "financial innovation" such as credit default swaps and crypto until there is an implosion of bankruptcies resulting in Ma and Pa losing their house. Yes, fertile ground for examination. But we are not going to do it. Onward elsewhere to another digression.

Do you see all those people making millions on bitcoin pizzas, krugerrands, and collectible plates from the Franklin mint? (According to Wikipedia, *[The Franklin Mint] was later acquired by Retail E-commerce Ventures (REV) in July 2020, a holding company that was founded by former NASA scientist Alex Mehr and his business partner, serial entrepreneur Tai Lopez.* But that is a sidebar, we must hasten back to our digression.)

I know I have, late at night, rued all those opportunities missed to get in on the ground floor of Apple, Google, and the Tickle Me Elmo craze. Why should I not be able to profit from what I know? And what do I know? Financial penalties for banks—I mean, have you been reading along or are you just flipping around looking for the pictures? It's like half the book is a listing of fines and settlements. Saved me a lot of writing all those quotes from regulators.

But back to me, in my fugue state, ruminating on the value of penalties. There must be an opportunity to leverage that information, or alpha, as they call it in the "trade." Let me get in on some of that sweet hedging and hawing funding. The idea is: companies that get fined must have some underlying weakness and the price of their stock should reflect that. Is there a possible exchange traded fund (the fancy new form of mutual funds) to be had?

Stock price is supposed to be representative of corporate value, and a company getting thrown in jail is not valuable, right? There's all this stuff going on now about environmental, social, governance, ESG they call it. Companies that do good in the world are potentially worth more. What could be more good than not committing crimes?

Late into the early morning hours and through the next several days I began researching. I used the website *Good Jobs First* for their, frankly, amazing list of violations, Yahoo! Finance to gather the historical stock prices, and a sprinkling of Python, Jupyter notebooks, and pandas software to do me some data science.

I found 1,120 records of fines over $1,000,000 of public companies between January 2010 and July 2022. That's a total of $201,971,673,913 in cash paid out by banks. That must have really hit the shareholder value. I chose to look at the price of the stock the day before the announcement of the fine and the day after.

I selected the day after because my stock analysis friends tell me that the markets are efficient and information is priced in quickly. A day may even be too long. And I picked the day before as a starting point because no one should have known that a fine was coming, or what the total amount of fine would be. If someone was aware of the details before it was made officially public, that would have been what's known as material nonpublic information (MNPI). Trading on MNPI, as the cool kids call it, is illegal. And, before you compliance nerds correct me, it is also a violation of confidential supervisory information rules. So I'm going to have to assume that everyone was playing with their hands above the card table—if they weren't that probably just makes my analysis even less palatable.

By now you've already skipped ahead to the picture, just like I knew you would, but allow me the big reveal. Aaaaaaand here it is … .

U.S. Bank Fines and Settlements over $1 Million January 2010 to July 2022
Impact on Stock Price

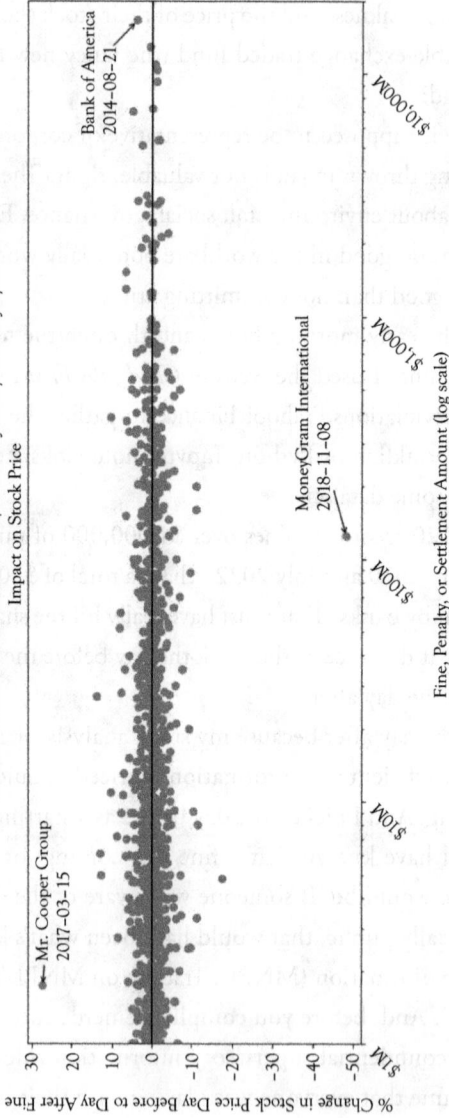

Bank of America
2014–08–21

MoneyGram International
2018–11–08

Mr. Cooper Group
2017–03–15

% Change in Stock Price Day Before to Day After Fine

30 20 10 0 –10 –20 –30 –40 –50

$1M $10M $100M $1,000M $10,000M

Fine, Penalty, or Settlement Amount (log scale)

First, this is a logarithmic graph, meaning the x-axis jumps by an order of magnitude at every major tick mark. I did this so you could see more of the dots. A fine of a billion dollars is, per math I'm told, a thousand times larger than a million. In astronomical terms, that's like the distance between Earth and the Sun versus the hypothesized home of comets, the Oort cloud and the Sun, which is very very very far. Without a log scale, most of the dots would be clustered by the y-axis like kittens near a warm fire. Thus, you should not lose sight of the fact that dots above 100 million and 1 billion are vastly larger in terms of cash money.

Second, you may look at this and say, most stocks changed up or down less than 10 percent, but that's an artifact of the graphic and dots overlapping. About 467 or 42 percent of the prices changed less than 1 percent up or down—after a fine of more than $1,000,000, and often, as we said, a lot lot lot more, was announced.

The full statistical breakdown is provided as follows, but it's easy to sum up: nada. Some stocks went up, some went down, on average, nearly zero change in value. This may affect your view of the stock market being rational, or it may influence your view on the impact of regulatory actions on company behavior, or both, I don't know how jaded you already were.

% Change	
Count of fines	1,120
Mean	0.04
Standard deviation	3.15
25%	−1.19
50%	0.00
75%	+1.27

For deeper insight, let's examine the outliers, the biggest gain, the biggest loss, and the biggest fine. Let's start at the top, in terms of gains at least, Mr. Cooper, which is really the company's name, who saw their stock rise by 27 percent on March 15, 2017 as it was announced:

CFPB Takes Action Against Nationstar Mortgage for Flawed Mortgage Loan Reporting: Bureau's $1.75 Million Civil Penalty for Persistent and Substantial Reporting Errors is the CFPB's

Largest Penalty to Date for HMDA [Home Mortgage Disclosure Act] Violations.

Hang on, that says Nationstar Mortgage and not the strangest name in home finance, Mr. Cooper. Well, that's because they changed it. Per their press release on May 2, 2017:

DALLAS—(BUSINESS WIRE)—Nationstar Mortgage Holdings Inc. (NYSE: NSM) ("Nationstar") today announced that it will officially rebrand its operating company, Nationstar Mortgage LLC, to "Mr. Cooper" in August. The brand name change is a significant step forward in the company's two-year transformation to make homeownership more rewarding and less worrisome for its nearly 3 million customers.

Was that really the best they could do naming their company? Is it supposed to be friendly? Human face on giant company? Is anyone else thinking about D. B. Cooper, the 1971 bank thief, who leapt out of a plane with $200,000 in $20 bills and was never seen again? And although the timing does look a little odd, 17 days after the fine, to be fair, this name change was apparently in the works for several years—several years to come up with Mr. Cooper? Also the press release says nothing about HMDA or the Reg C violation.

There's also nothing in the 2nd quarter report, but the annual report sure has something, right? It was the biggest HMDA blah blah blah, yes? Here's the homespun cover of said report.

On page 10 it says how they are one of the *best* mortgage companies:

We just received Fannie Mae's highest level of performance recognition—the Five STAR designation—for the fourth year running thanks to their dedication and this award is yet another reflection of our employees' complete dedication, to providing an impressive customer experience.

But it does mention on page 36:

These matters include investigations by the Consumer Financial Protection Bureau, the Securities and Exchange Commission, the Executive

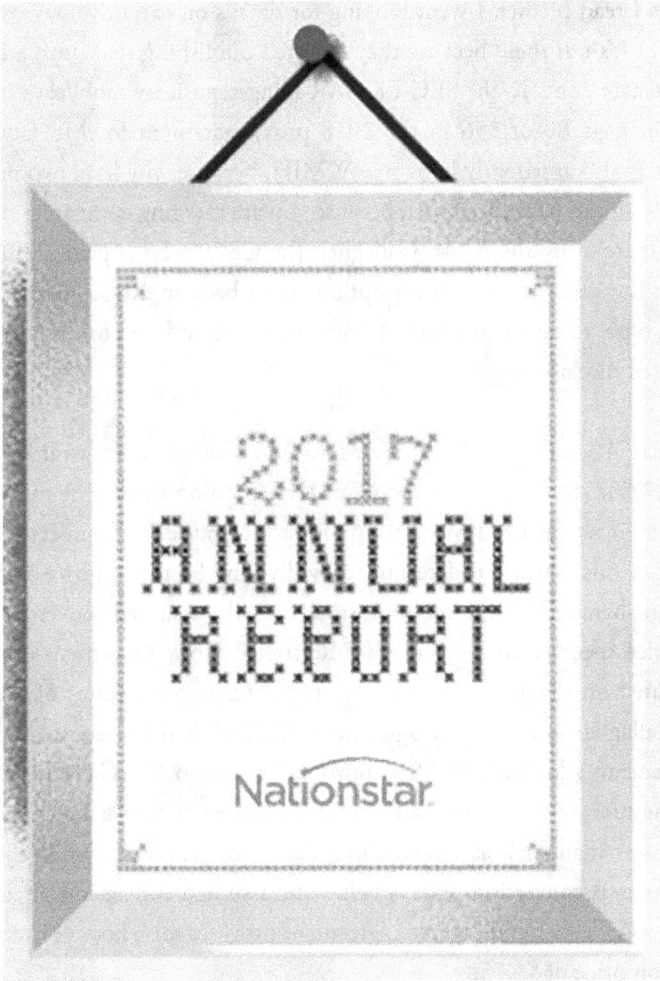

Office of the United States Trustees, the Department of Justice, the U.S. Department of Housing and Urban Development, the multistate coalition of mortgage banking regulators, various State Attorneys General, and the New York Department of Financial Services.

But that's just one of several pages of "other" risks, which is, itself, just part of the overall risk section that is 20 pages long. Further on we get to revenue, which was $1.65 billion for 2017. Is it worth pointing out this is 94.3 times the size of the CFPB fine? Maybe.

As I read further, I went looking for details on executive pay, as you do, but it's not there because they deferred publishing that until a 2018 proxy statement. To the SEC-EDGAR-filing-repository mobile!

On page 80 of 356 in the 2018 proxy statement for Mr. Cooper, which is also apparently known as WMIH, because why have two names when you can have three, well because you are merging companies, that's why, there's this about Mr. Gallagher, the CEO, who is paid $500,000 a year but also has some stock options from back in 2015. Here it is in small type, to give you a feel of how much they wanted to disclose this required disclosure:

> May 15, 2015, WMIH issued to Mr. Gallagher an award of 1,777,778 restricted shares of WMIH common stock. The number of shares of WMIH common stock granted in connection with this award was determined by dividing $4 million by $2.25 per share of WMIH common stock (i.e., the assumed conversion price specified in the Gallagher Restricted Stock Agreement executed on the grant date); however, pursuant to the terms of the Gallagher employment agreement, WMIH will be required to issue an additional 507,936 restricted shares to Mr. Gallagher if the merger is consummated since the Series B conversion price is less than such assumed conversion price. However, while the Series B conversion price is below the assumed conversion price, the Gallagher employment agreement provides for a floor conversion price of $1.75.

When the stock went from $13.80 to $16.80—let's call him Mr. G. from now on, it's more homey, like the company or the cool English teacher who takes time to remember all the student's dog's names—Mr. G. made either an additional $5,333,334 or $6,857,142, depending if the merger went through (it did). The total value of his shares would have been approximately $38,399,995 and 20 cents. We could point out how this is 20 times the size of the CFPB fine, but we won't, and not just because it's 21.9428544 times the size of the fine. We also won't point out that Mr. F., the chief operation officer, had been given identical stock options either because there's more to the story.

Maybe we should focus our attention that a few months later on December 4, 2017:

> SACRAMENTO—*The California Department of Business Oversight (DBO) today announced that Nationstar Mortgage, doing business as Mr. Cooper, has agreed to pay more than $9.2 million in refunds and penalties to resolve allegations that the Texas-based mortgage lender and servicer overcharged borrowers and failed to properly investigate consumer complaints.*
>
> *"You don't get to take advantage of consumers in California," DBO Commissioner Jan Lynn Owen said. "With this settlement (PDF), the DBO has secured millions in refunds for borrowers, penalties to discourage future violations, and ongoing independent audits to monitor Nationstar's compliance with California law."*

Or that on April 11, 2018:

> *Albany, NY—Financial Services Superintendent Maria T. Vullo today announced that the Department of Financial Services (DFS) has fined Nationstar Mortgage LLC $5 million for violations of New York State Banking Law, stemming from the company's failure to develop effective, scalable controls that could keep pace with its rapid growth. As a result of DFS examinations, Nationstar has made restitution of $7 million to New York borrowers. Under the consent order with DFS, Nationstar will also donate $5 million in residential real property or first-lien mortgages to one or more nonprofit organizations to assist in the rehabilitation of vacant and abandoned properties.*

Or this on December 7, 2020:

> *Today the Consumer Financial Protection Bureau (Bureau) filed a complaint and proposed stipulated judgment and order against Nationstar Mortgage, LLC, which does business as Mr. Cooper (Nationstar). The Bureau's action is part of a coordinated effort between the Bureau, a multistate group of state attorneys general, and state bank regulators. The Bureau alleges that Nationstar violated multiple Federal consumer financial laws, causing substantial harm to the borrowers whose mortgage loans it serviced, including distressed homeowners.*

Nationstar is one of the nation's largest mortgage servicers and the largest nonbank mortgage servicer in the United States. The proposed judgment and order, if entered by the court, would require Nationstar to pay approximately $73 million in redress to more than 40,000 harmed borrowers.

It would also require Nationstar to pay a $1.5 million civil penalty to the Bureau. Attorneys general from all 50 states and the District of Columbia and bank regulators from 53 jurisdictions covering 48 states and Puerto Rico, the Virgin Islands, and the District of Columbia have also settled with Nationstar today and their settlements are reflected in separate actions, concurrently filed in the United States District Court for the District of Columbia.

Look at all those angry jurisdictions making bad Mr. Cooper pay up. They weren't alone. In a separate action from the U.S. DOJ, also on December 7, 2020 (a day that will live in infamy?)

The Department of Justice's U.S. Trustee Program (USTP announced today that it has entered into national agreements with three mortgage servicers to address past mortgage servicing deficiencies impacting homeowners in bankruptcy.

[...]

Nationstar has provided more than $40 million in credits and refunds. U.S. Bank has, or will, provide at least $29 million in credits and refunds, and has waived approximately $43 million in fees and charges across its mortgage servicing portfolio, including for borrowers in bankruptcy. PNC provided close to $5 million in credits and refunds, as well as additional remediation in the form of lien releases and debt forgiveness.

And here's that story I promised: the stock price had nothing to do with the fines. Here are all the fines—over $1 million, we won't bother with the $500,000 from Massachusetts or the $760,000 from Maryland, or the $9,200 from Rhode Island, really Rhode Island? $9,200? Are there not enough jokes about how small you are?

Mr. Cooper almost certainly spent more than $9,200 designing this icon from their website:

Fine	Date	%Δ Stock Price
$1,750,000	2017-03-15	+27.27
$9,118,784	2017-12-04	−10.42
$17,000,000	2018-04-11	+0.69
$74,500,000	2020-12-07	+2.20
$40,000,000	2020-12-07	+2.20
$142,368,784		Total

The total fine is almost $90,000,000 less than Mr. Cooper's interest income from 2021, which was $231,000,000. That is the money earned on money that was sitting there doing nothing other than sloughing off more money from the intrinsic nature of being money in bank accounts.

The *Motley Fool* investment advice site had this to say about the future value of the company on May 31, 2022, with nary a mention of a history of fines and settlements:

Stock in Mr. Cooper has far outperformed its peers so far in 2022. Mortgage servicing is an asset that increases in value as rates rise. Motley Fool Issues Rare "All In" Buy Alert.

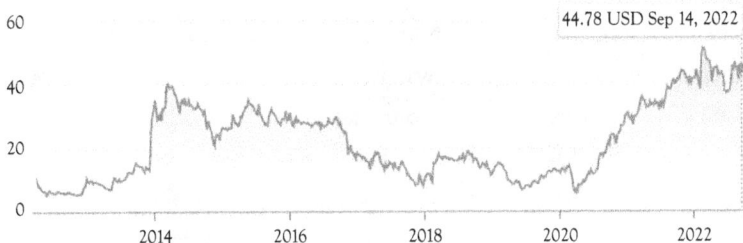

Mr. Cooper Stock Performance

And here's where the stock is as I write this. Somewhere Mr. G. and Mr. F. are doing all right.

Next up, MoneyGram. Here again is the *Motley Fool* giving us stories to explain the whirligig machine that is the stock market:

> *Shares of MoneyGram International (NASDAQ: MGI) are plunging in active trading today, declining by more than 44 percent as of 3:40 p.m. EST.*
>
> *Wall Street is turning on the stock after it issued disappointing guidance for the remainder of 2018 and separately announced a $125 million settlement with the Federal Trade Commission and Department of Justice over its failure to stamp out fraudulent uses of money transfers.*

Poor MoneyGram, they ended the day at 48 percent loss, although I'm not sure that management could have predicted that the Federal trade commission (FTC) and DOJ fine would be a significant cause. They had been hit with $100 million six years earlier—almost to the day! —but that only dropped the stock 6 percent. Perhaps it had more to do with that *disappointing guidance?*

Fine	Date	%Δ Stock Price
$4,500,000	2011-05-20	−2.41
$100,000,000	2012-11-09	−6.02
$13,000,000	2016-02-11	+7.03
$125,000,000	2018-11-08	−48.17
$8,250,000	2022-03-16	−0.84
$250,750,000	Total	

Then again, maybe it has nothing to do with either of those things because it was in the deep, er, water already after it lost a ton of money playing with mortgage-backed securities in 2007, which was when the, what was it, yes, I remember now, mortgage-backed securities TNT pile exploded and the entire financial market went into free fall.

Apparently MoneyGram sold everything at a huge loss, and their attempt to write their $540 million loss off their taxes was met by the

IRS with, I am assuming, amusement of the kind only an IRS agent can muster—meaning they took MoneyGram to tax court and beat them and then to appeals court and plastered them again. Remember when we earlier discussed how the law is open to debate? That's far less true in tax court and this is a picture of an IRS agent smiling about it: 😎.

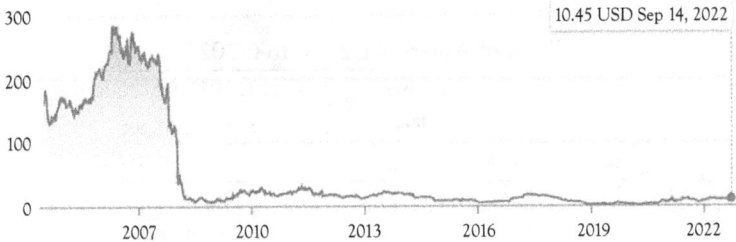

MoneyGram Stock Performance

The hits that came from regulators during the period I was analyzing, 2010 to 2022, were long after the company was essentially a pinata for takeovers and crypto schemes. Here's the *Wall Street Journal* in February 2021 about the strange and strained relationship with crypto firm Ripple falling apart.

> *MoneyGram, a Dallas-based money-transfer company, this week said it suspended its partnership with Ripple in December after securities regulators sued Ripple for violating investor protection laws.*
>
> *[...]*
>
> *Last year, MoneyGram received $38 million in net market development fees from Ripple, representing about 15 percent of the company's adjusted earnings before interest, taxes, depreciation and amortization. But after the lawsuit was filed, the company said it faced logistical challenges in using the platform as well as legal and reputational risks.*

Bank of America is next on our hit parade. But what's the point? Bank of America has been fined, since January 2010, and counting only those fines over $1 million, 113 times for a total of $63,785,277,402. The maximum stock price change was −6.7 percent on the down and +8.9 percent on the up. The average was +0.27 percent.

Are you concerned I've been too lax about the fines by focusing only above $1 million? Let's be extra picayune and get every last drop, including $5,287 in September 2010 for wage and hour violations in Georgia. All together we will get another $7.5 million drop of water in this reservoir of penalties. The new total is: $63,792,861,406. Over the same period, BofA had revenue of $1,101,050,000,000.

Bank of America 1/2010 to 6/2022	
Revenue	$1,101,050,000,000
Fines	$63,792,861,406
Fines as % of Revenue	5.8%

The total fines paid by Bank of America (ticker BAC) versus its revenues for a 12 ½ year period was 5.8 percent. Certainly money they would have preferred not to have paid and reputational damage they would rather have avoided, but could they afford it? Could they have given fewer raises to tellers, told employees to pay for their own Christmas parties, given a little less to charitable causes, and written some of this off on their taxes? You know the answer to both questions: yes.

And how did the stock do otherwise? Pretty good. Macro trends around the entire market have affected it in the summer of 2022, but in general, pretty good. I chose this graph because it has all those little "D"s at the bottom. Those are dividends. If you had bought BAC at the start of this period that would see almost $64 billion in fines, and sold the day I wrote this, you would have doubled your money, and gotten all those sweet, sweet "D"s.

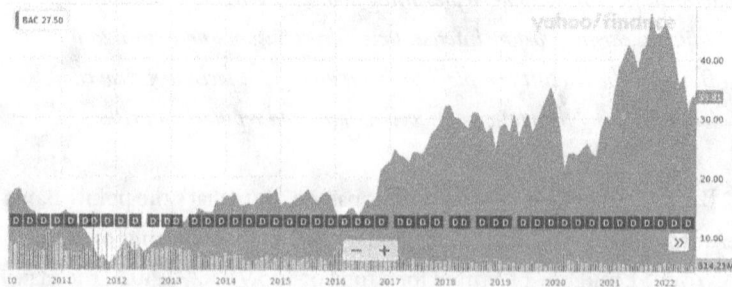

BAC Stock Price

Here's some more data on all of the fines and penalties between 2010 and July 2022 and how much of revenue they represent.

U.S. Bank Fines and Settlements over $10 Million
January 2010 to July 2022
Cumulative Fines as % of Revenue

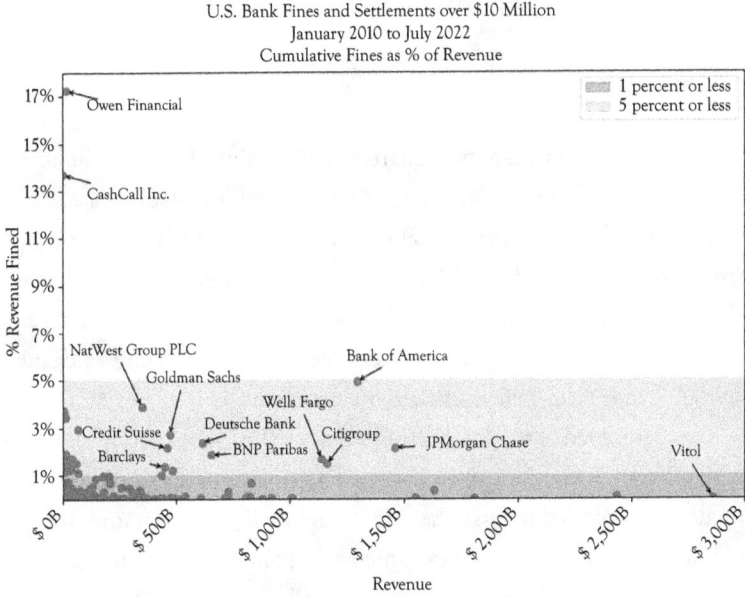

And, to save you trying to triangulate all of this with a ruler and protractors, here are the top 10 fines in table form:

	Top 10 Bank Fines as a % of Revenue Cumulative January 2010 to July 2022			
Rank	Company	Revenue	Fines	%
1	Bank of America	$ 1,295B	$ 63.8B	4.93
2	JPMorgan Chase	$ 1,462B	$ 31.3B	2.14
3	Wells Fargo	$ 1,139B	$ 18.7B	1.65
4	Citigroup	$ 1,161B	$ 16.9B	1.45
5	Deutsche Bank	$ 614B	$ 14.5B	2.37
6	NatWest Group PLC	$ 347B	$ 13.5B	3.89
7	Goldman Sachs	$ 470B	$ 12.7B	2.7
8	NP Paribas	$ 654B	$ 12.1B	1.86
9	Credit Suisse	$ 458B	$ 9.9B	2.15
10	Barclays	$ 447B	$ 6.0B	1.34

And what about everyone else? Of the 154 companies I looked at over that time frame here's the punchline:

Total Fines	$262,064,573,883
Total Revenue	$46,238,773,345,452
%	0.57

That's a bit less than two quarters and a dime for every hundred dollars of top of the line income for the companies I looked at. A full 45 percent of the companies, 69 of them, paid less than a tenth of a percent of revenue in fines. That's a mere two jitneys for every hundred simoleons—the Internet claims a "jitney" is slang for a nickel—don't say I never told you anything useful. Regardless, that's not going to change any ticker tape feeds being watched by men with top hats and monocles.

I am reminded of the camera shops that used to populate Time Square in New York City in the 1990s. They had huge signs in the windows offering deals in bold red letters. They were brightly lit, like operating rooms, with long counters full of fancy cameras, but almost no one inside other than the six guys behind the counter who all shared a penchant for gold necklaces and seemed ready to sell your kidney if you stood still too long.

They seemed to be scams, all of them, and they were. My sister tried to buy some polaroid film and they convinced her she needed a battery pack to use the film. She did not. But, unsure at the time, she bought it. And here's the thing, they were in business for years. Years. They never made a customer happy, but they didn't have to. This was NYC and tourists, who needed film, or a camera, or mistakenly walked in thinking they could get the deal on the sign, were in endless supply—essentially a camera shop Ponzi with new money always there to prop up the enterprise.

A company's primary goal is to make money. This is drilled into all our heads by every talking head on TV or Internet personas: stockholder value. If a customer happens to be satisfied as a result or if a product works as designed and does not melt the skin of your inner thigh or leave you without a home or not break the law, well, that's a side benefit—good for us—as long as we also made money.

Think about what that does to the rest of the industry. If everyone speeds, and only a few people get tickets, and those tickets aren't terribly expensive, what incentive does anyone have to drive the speed limit? What rating will you give an Uber driver who drives the speed limit? What trucking company can afford to make its drivers obey the speed limit? And how can you compete if other companies gain market share and loyal customers while pushing beyond the boundaries of what is acceptable?

Bank of America isn't an anomaly. Mr. G. and Mr. F. aren't bad apples. I want you to stop thinking about bad apples and start thinking about a system where following the law is not only open to interpretation, but the more you try to "color inside the lines" of what is legal, the harder it is to make money in a financial system where everyone is speeding. How can you afford not to drive as fast as you think is possible—hoping you're not the one getting the ticket? But if you do, it's not that bad, so hey, keep on pressing that gas pedal. Consider: there were no reputable camera shops in Times Square. They couldn't afford to compete.

What we have seen here is that regulation and regulators' ability to improve Compliance, at least where it affects company and shareholder value, is a nonentity. Investors through their actions in the market obviously know this, or it would show up in the numbers—which show no correlation between fines and share value.

Moreover, customers of banks are notoriously "sticky." I do not mean to imply they are covered with jam, what they do on their own time is their business. But many people stay with the same bank for decades, if not their entire lives. If a customer isn't directly harmed by the actions related to a given fine, they tend to stay put, which provides another nonincentive to comply—and instead compels banks to open as many branches as they can to be in the literal line of sight when a customer is born figuratively or, I suppose, literally. My son, as an example, got his first account at a branch on the route between the hospital and home. No, not that day, I'm not a monster, and I needed a nap, so did my wife, but when that passbook was stamped (digitally! I'm not a luddite either, sheesh, judgmental much?) he wasn't walking yet.

What then can be done?

CHAPTER 6

A Compliance Manifesto

Remember back to the start of this book? Almost half a billion dollars in fines for financial companies. Then we looked at the billions spent by banks on Compliance departments. And then we looked at how much money that is versus their total income. And the question *Why isn't it solved? Why do banks keep getting fined?* seemed to answer itself: banks don't comply with the law because they don't need to. Fundamentally the profit in finance is on the edge of legality, so scooting up to, or over it, is worth the fines to acquire the business, and then clean up the mess later, after the cash is in the vault.

Banks create Compliance departments, staff them as regulatory pressure increases, and disband them when the regulators lift consent orders. In between those dates, the Compliance department spins up thousands of pages of policies, procedures, tests, risk assessments, and project plans, spends millions buying and building computer systems, and achieves next to nothing material in terms of actual change. At the same time, the current regulatory action gets far enough along to be lifted long enough for the cycle to repeat. Let's call it Compliance-washing. And the total cost versus the opportunities of market share for a few fake accounts or fudged disclosures or laundered drug money does not move the bottom line enough to stop the rinse, spin, repeat.

I would like this to stop. And, with all honesty, most executives and employees at financial institutions want it to stop also. I've made the point that the endemic criminality of finance isn't the fault of a "few bad apples." The system is structured to reward and enable misbehavior. But that doesn't mean people like it—or that a majority likes it. The opposite is true. Most people would like everyone to be going the speed limit, including themselves. Most people feel exhausted and demoralized that the only way to survive is by pushing the boundaries of legality every day. Most people want the status quo to change.

I have witnessed multiple banks go through this cycle. They hire everyone from all the other banks with the word "Compliance" anywhere on their resume, then, after scapegoating some tranche of Compliance executives—probably the CCO themselves more than once—move Compliance to Legal, then to Risk, then to the CCO, pleading that *now we've got it!* At some point the regulators accept a plan and it's back to business as usual.

Having been part of that laundry cycle, I've had enough vertigo. I therefore present my humble manifesto for fixing Compliance. Consider these my theses nailed to the church door.[1]

Thesis 1. Authority of Compliance
Increase Compliance's authority and reorganize to reduce the internal political pressure to "not rock the boat."

Thesis 2. Ethics Over Law
Focus policy and training on ethics and job-related requirements to drive the right behaviors.

Thesis 3. Automation through Data
Automate Compliance management and reporting with improved technology and linked data.

Thesis 4. Effective External Oversight
Make regulatory oversight effective with meaningful penalties and external oversight.

Let's dive into each of these and see how they might be implemented.

Thesis 1. Authority of Compliance

Increase Compliance's authority and reorganize to reduce the internal political pressure to "not rock the boat."

There's a lot of talk in banks about the "stature" of Compliance. But Compliance departments report to the GC or the chief risk officer (CRO), or worse to divisional heads GCs or CROs, or even worse than that to divisional business heads. This means that the CCO has a boss who can

---

[1] These my theses? Thesis plural is very weird.

be asked to "tell Compliance to back off." Also, it usually means that the CCO is not on the senior most Executive or Operating Committee of the firm. How can you have "stature" when you are only invited to ExCo meetings as a guest who has to leave when your 10-minute presentation time is up?

Let's fix this.

End the Three Lines of Defense

The three lines of defense model causes duplication of efforts among the frontline business, Compliance, Legal, Testing (if you have a separate Testing department, which some banks do have), and Audit. Who needs to know the requirements of the law and check that the controls are in place? In the three lines model, everyone does, and so everyone hires staff.

More cooks here are not making a better meal—instead they are making multiple meals that have to be compared against each other. People assume that the Swiss cheese model will catch problems if they fall through any given one of those checks. But instead this leads to testing, assessment, and audit fatigue where red flags get buried under make-work multiple reports.

There is no regulatory requirement for three lines of defense. There is no proven benefit. There are only checkers checking checkers. So stop it.

What then to do with the Compliance department?

Split Compliance Into Oversight and Operations

As we have discussed, Compliance has two primary tasks. One is to provide oversight of the business by monitoring and reporting how the business is designing and enforcing regulatory-related controls.

The second is to enforce some of these controls directly, such as checking transactions for activity that might indicate money laundering; reviewing marketing literature to make sure it complies with requirements to disclose fees; or seeking licenses to operate in a state or country.

Let's call these two groups Compliance Oversight and Compliance Operations, and begin with reorganizing the latter.

Compliance Operations Moves to the Business

The operations function fits best in the business itself. Knowing and implementing the regulatory requirements is a business function. The fact that it is about regulation doesn't mean it should be in a separate department. It is operational work no different than opening accounts, receiving payments, or making loans. In fact, it is exactly that work—so move the tasks and people to the business.

Compliance Oversight Reports to the Board of Directors

In my first draft I had Compliance Oversight reporting to the CEO. But I realized that's not sufficient. It would get the CCO a seat at the top ExCo, but it would still be among peers, and peers who run businesses have more political pull than those who do not.

Audit shares the same concerns as Compliance. Cooked bookkeeping is also illegal, has fuzzy boundaries for what is exactly legit and is born of the same desires and has some of the same benefits as any other noncompliance.[2]

For this reason, namely that calling out illegal activity needs a cop as highly placed as the potential criminals, Audit is seen as having to report to the board of directors and to be a peer of the CEO themselves.

It is also worth noting that the BSA/AML officer already reports to the board of directors and that this is required by law. This is the person charged with owning the AML program at a bank and it is a regulatory mandated position. Technically, the BSA/AML officer is required to make an annual report to the board and to be approved in their position by the board, but not be actually managed as an employee of the board. Instead the BSA/AML officer usually reports to the CCO, who may be one in the same person or not. If they are different people, it makes it sort of weird

---

[2] Enron, WorldCom, Tyco, Parmalat, and many other names you may have seen were big accounting scandals. But this book is about regulatory compliance, so if you don't know about them, no worries. I'm sure you can easily Google some more. The point is that Audit and Compliance are more akin than not. That's why this is a footnote.

that the more junior employee has to report to the board, but the CCO doesn't (at least not by law).

Compliance should be afforded the same status as Audit and the CCO should report to the board. This also fixes the strangeness of the BSA/AML officer having a higher management responsibility from the CCO. If you wanted to go so far as to combine them into one department, that would be fine also.

As a side note, auditing of Compliance is something that also happens. Yes, really. And it's just another dumb result of the three lines of defense structure. Let's stop that too, please.

Thesis 2. Ethics Over Law

Focus policy and training on ethics and job-related requirements to drive the right behaviors.

As I hope I've made clear, there's a distinction between the "law" and what a reasonable person might consider to be ethical behavior. The gap between the two being careful didactic argumentation applied with a mercenary mindset. One solution here is to not try to color so close to the line.

For example, Reg Z, Truth in Lending, allows a "right to rescind" for some personal mortgages. The idea being that sometimes people get pressured into a refinance and maybe, given a few days to think it over, realize they don't want to do the deal.

The rescission rules are complex. You have until midnight on the third business day and the mortgage, generally, must be secured by your primary residence, not being issued by your current lender, and not being used to buy your home. In addition, there is a clause where if the lender doesn't provide the required disclosures, the customer can initiate a rescission within three years of the mortgage.

Just looking at the first condition, three days, as we discussed earlier, defining a "business day" is not cut and dried and you can imagine the chaos possible. But, surprisingly, the big issue here has been the three years thing. Jesinoski et ux. v. Countrywide Home Loans, Inc., et al. got all the way to the U.S. Supreme Court.

The state and appellate courts had sided with Countrywide. The case initial was about whether the bank had given two or four copies of the required disclosures. The Jesinoskis argued that they should have gotten four (two each) and the bank said, no, only two. The Eighth Circuit Court agreed with the bank and said the copies thing was "argument as a tortured attempt to create an ambiguity where none exists." That's some stiff medicine, but the Jesinoskis appealed to the top court in the land.

At the Supreme Court, the case somehow transformed to be about the question: can the borrower initiate rescission by sending a notice to the bank or do they have to file a lawsuit? The bank said a lawsuit was required. The Court, 9–0 disagreed. The Jesinoskis could rescind their loan. By the way, I can't figure out if they only had to return the principal amount or what happened to several years of interest—maybe you have better Google mojo than me?

A few things to note here:

- In 2003, Countrywide stock was up 23,000 percent. At the time the CEO, Angelo Mozilo, was paid $33 million dollars.
- Angelo, liked to say, "You need to make dust or eat dust, and I don't like eating dust."
- In 2006, Angelo said one of their mortgage products, "The 100 percent loan-to-value subprime product is 'the most dangerous product in existence and there can be nothing more toxic and therefore requires that no deviation from guidelines be permitted irrespective of the circumstances.'"
- In another 2006 e-mail, Angelo also said he "personally observed a serious lack of compliance within our origination system as it relates to documentation and generally a deterioration in the quality of loans."
- The Jesinoski's loan in 2007 was $611,000.
- One year later, in 2008, Countrywide imploded during the mortgage crisis because they had pressed the edges of legality in the subprime mortgage market.
- The case lasted almost six years from February 2010 until it was decided (at the Supreme Court) in December 2015.

TL/DR: A mortgage lender ripped off consumers while making massive profits, knew it was pushing the boundaries to do so, and would have kept chugging along if the whole market hadn't imploded.

Here's my suggestion. Don't fight customers over the details and don't make toxic products in the first place. Countrywide internal policy on mortgages could have said:

> Hey, Reg Z gives 3 days to rescind and 3 years if we mess up the disclosures. How about we give people a week to decide? Or how about we just let people rescind for 3 years? Would that be the right thing to do? What might that cost us? Would it maybe save us money by not having to litigate a $611,000 loan all the way to the Supreme Court? Can someone remind me what an hour of outside counsel's time costs us?

Let's continue this idea by rethinking one of the Compliance pillars: corporate policy with a clean slate.

One Policy: Code of Conduct

Given that the primary purpose of policy is to state the ethical boundaries of behavior as defined by management, there's only one policy needed: a clear and concise Code of Conduct that lays out what acceptable behavior is and what is not.

Policy is what everyone in the company should be reading, including the CEO and board of directors. Currently, banks have dozens or hundreds of policies. Nobody can read or remember all of them. The single Code solves this problem.

Employees don't need to know the details of laws or regulations on products they don't deal with, but everyone needs to know what's right from wrong. In other words, leave the law out of your Code of Conduct. It's about what the company should do irrespective of the external rule book.

The details of how to handle specific regulations belong in the procedures (more on them in the next section). But as one example, my proposed change to recission: three days regulatory requirement being relaxed to one week or to just let people have a full three years to rescind, that goes in the mortgage procedures.

So what does a good Code of Conduct look like? *We do not harm customers*[3] is a good first sentence. Here are some more:

- *We comply with the spirit and letter of regulations and, whenever practical, provide more flexibility to customers than required by law.*
- *When determining business decisions, we should act as if the discussion and option chosen were to be made public today or at a later point in time.*
- *We disclose all risks to customers with easy to understand, plain language disclosures.*
- *We do not self-deal. That is, we do not take positions in the market where we stand to gain if our customers lose.*
- *We respect our employees and our customers equally.*
- *Employees who break our policies or the law are subject to termination and we will report their activity to the appropriate regulatory authority.*
- *We protect whistleblowers.*

Do these seem scarily reasonable? Reasonable in that people probably already thought banks did this kind of stuff, at least in principle; and scary because, oh my, what if we had to live ethically and at the same time try to make money? I suggest it's worth trying. And if you do, feel free to copy these policy statements and, may I propose even further, that you post them on your website and in every branch?

Two Training Courses: Code of Conduct and Job Specific

Training is another Compliance pillar and closely related to policy. Training is about being sure your staff know what is expected of them. This means they should know the Code of Conduct and be able to operate the bank accordingly.

---

[3] That's the title of the book again!

As we have seen, training tends to devolve into something played in a web browser behind Microsoft Outlook and clicked on just enough to get to the end. Let's move beyond this. Training should be two courses only: Code of Conduct and job specific.

Training number one, the Code of Conduct, as discussed previously, is the center of the ethical framework of the firm. Training here is non-negotiable and should be given every year, in person, test at the end, have to pass it to go back to work, no exceptions, board of directors included.

Training number two is focused on how to do a given job. This would be training directly connected to the procedures for that role—say processing payments, doing investment banking, handling complaints on mortgages, marketing commercial loans, and so on. More on the following procedures. And since there's really not a lot more to say about training—because it really can be this simple—let's move on to those pillars, which we will seek to improve using technology.

Thesis 3. Automate Through Data

Automate Compliance management and reporting with improved technology and linked data.

I've discussed about what's wrong with GRC systems. Now for my suggestions. Let's start with the laws, rules, regulations, procedures, controls, and processes, and then move on to how we test and risk assess from that. Lastly, we will cover my "Google for Compliance."

Laws, Rules, Regulations, Procedures, Controls, and Processes

The foundation of Compliance is the law. So we should have a list of them. You can call it a law library, but a list of relevant laws, rules, and regulations is fine.[4] That list should have standardized citations to the

---

[4] I keep referring to laws, rules, and regulations as three things. Technically, to a lawyer, they are three things. Or maybe more if you consider proposed laws and regulations also. Essentially the law is made by a legislative body, like the Congress. The regulation is created by an agency, such as the Fed in response to the law. And a rule is made by a nongovernment regulator such as FINRA. Or, the rule is part of the regulation. The terms are fuzzy. Like a lawyer in a snuggie.

actual law so it can be easily looked up by procedure writers and tracked for changes.

Next we need a library of procedures. Procedures document how a company operates, and you can have as many or few as you like. However, for anything with a legal requirement, there should be at least one procedure. The procedures don't need to be all at the same level of detail, but they should all be easy to find and you should have a list of them.[5]

Procedures need to be linked to the laws. This can be done as simply having footnotes in the procedures where the law applies, or with some more advanced document management system. Either is fine. The key is that the link from the procedures to the laws is done within the procedures by the procedure writers. This is for a few reasons:

1. Procedures are the heart of the bank's operations and should be the center of the data connections.
2. There's a lot more procedures than there are laws.
3. There's a lot more procedure writers than law librarians. Requiring all the procedure writers to put laws in their documents will result in better data quality than having a group of law librarians try to find, and maintain, the list of all relevant procedures.
4. Procedures change more as, or more, frequently than the laws change. Or rather, any change in law may cause a procedure change. But business process changes can also require a procedure update.
5. Testing, risk assessment, and auditing work off of the procedures. So having the laws listed there makes those tasks easier.
6. It's straightforward enough to reverse the links once they exist in the procedures to get a report of procedures linked to laws for regulatory change purposes.

---

[5] At this point, you will be unsurprised to learn that most, if not all, banks cannot easily lay hands on all their procedures. Much like the quote from Abraham Lincoln, they can find some of the procedures some of the time, but never all of the procedures all of the time. There are simply too many and in too many different systems.

Depending on the size and complexity of the company, there may also be a process library, a controls library, and an applications (technology systems) library. As we have discussed, I view procedures, processes, and controls as all the same thing. But if you want to have them separate, I will not argue with your desire to make a zillion little boxes—that's on you. Regardless though, all of these should also be linked in the procedures, if they exist.

You can also link the procedures to the Code of Conduct to indicate which parts of the Code they support. This is nice and makes everything super organized like a college roommate I once knew who ironed his khaki slacks and then hung them in order of beigeness. But it's not really necessary, because showing coverage of the law is through the procedures.

Here's a picture. I apologize for the clarity of it. We'll get to the "incl. metrics" thing in the next section on testing.

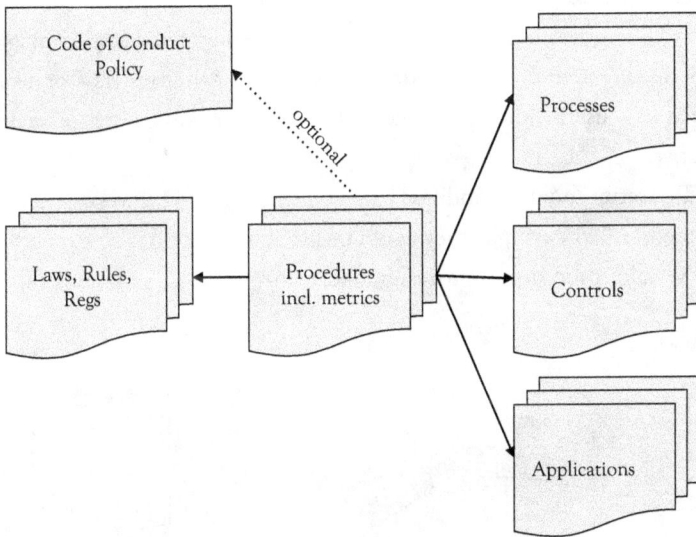

Automating Testing and Risk Assessment

Testing has two parts: testing the design of a control and separately testing the effectiveness.

For the design, the challenge currently is that it's hard to connect the dots between the legal requirements, the control, and associated applications and processes. In the picture above, we've just solved this. Figuring out if the procedure is designed to comply with the regulations and seeing if there are controls, processes, and applications is straightforward because it's built into the procedure writing from day one.

Part two, testing control effectiveness can be solved by adding a little bit to our procedures. Namely, specifying in the procedure what metrics to measure to determine how well a control is working right in the document itself. For example, the procedure on customer onboarding could identify metrics such as: how many customers began the onboarding, how many passed/failed KYC checks, how many were ultimately onboarded. And that the number onboarded should be the same as the number that passed the KYC checks.

Ideally those metrics are stored in a system somewhere, and the procedure tells you what system. If you have that, you can fully automate the effectiveness testing by gathering data from applications. If not, you will have to go collect the metrics as part of testing, but it's still going to be a much more straightforward process than having testers—or worse regulators—use their own judgment about what makes a given procedure effective.

This setup could be modified based on where you want to keep track of the metrics. For example, they could be listed in the controls or processes. As I've said, procedures, processes, and controls are all variations on the

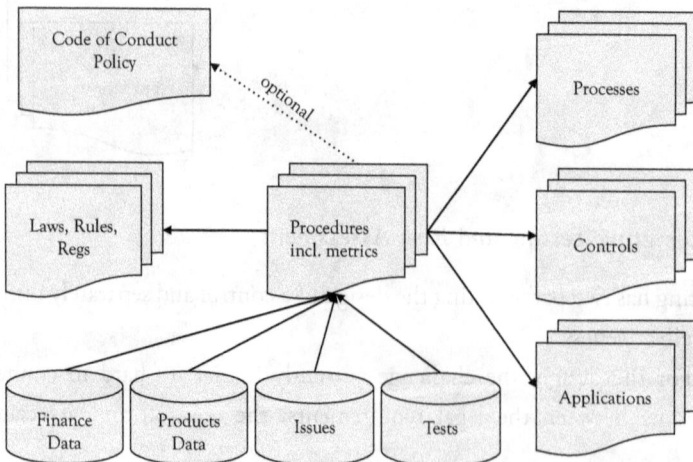

same dance, so put the pieces wherever you feel works best. The linkages will allow everything to be gathered together, and that's the main thing.

Now that we have testing working smoothly we can automate, or at least optimize, risk assessment. To do this, we will need to augment our picture a bit more. Specifically, we will want to connect finance, product, and issue data to the procedures. Technically, we already linked tests just a couple of paragraphs ago, but I didn't draw the picture until now. So here you go:

We've got the pieces assembled that we need to bake our risk assessment cake.[6] Recall that we need the following inputs: processes, control effectiveness, and inherent risk so that we can get an output of residual risk. Processes we have. Control effectiveness we have from testing and we can augment it with issue data. (You may have already used issue data in your testing, which is also fine–comme ci comme ça.)

Now for the trick, the flaming cherry on top as it were, inherent risk.[7] Instead of guessing what the impact might be, we have the financial data of products associated with a given procedure and therefore process. That's our inherent risk. To calculate residual risk, you create a standard function to convert overall control effectiveness (adjusted by the severity of related issues) to a number between 0 and 1. Then multiply that by the revenue. The final number is the amount you might lose if you don't get your controls in order.

Wait, hold on, it can't be that easy! I hear you say. *What about reputational impact or regulatory impact, that's subjective, we have to have meetings to discuss and waste everyone's time.* I both disagree with you and thank you for saying exactly the strawman argument I was looking for.

---

[6] I feel like things are getting a bit dry and technical, so apropos of nothing when I was a child I liked to bake cakes. I found an especially elaborate orange one in a Julia Child cookbook and I made it over the course of three days. No cake should take three days. It consisted of three individual cakes in a tower with cream filling in between. The batter recipe called for triple sec. I don't know how much but I used a whole bottle. The final cake was enormous with a texture akin to a cement block, but it packed a punch. I couldn't stomach it. But my mother froze the behemoth and when feeling a little bit in the need of a mood alteration would defrost a small hunk and have it with tea.

[7] I would not recommend lighting a match anywhere near that 100 proof orange cake I made.

The potential reputational or regulatory impact can always end up being 100 percent of the value of the product, or, worst case, the value of the entire company. This is because one bad story in the *New York Times* or regulatory action can turn any product, no matter how apparently dull into an inferno.[8] Witness the mortgage meltdown of the 2007 financial crisis. What's more dull than a mortgage?

And choosing the associated products' revenue as the base inherent risk, rather than the whole company's income, is good enough for getting people's attention in terms of calculating residual risk as a percentage of the income statement.

The benefit here is that business people will react much more predictably to numbers with dollar signs and the resultant potential monetary loss than to some super detailed checkerboard of red, green, and yellow. You could thank me now, but there's more good stuff to come. The "Google for Compliance" is up next.

Implementing a "Google for Compliance"

Author's note, May 2023: I wrote this section back in the distant past of 2022. In early 2023, ChatGPT emerged and many have claimed the world has changed forever. I can confirm that I am now paying $20 a month for access to ChatGPT 4 and use it regularly to "check" my homework in my Master of Computer Science studies at the University of Illinois, Urbana Champaign. And by check, I mean give me Python and JavaScript in a few seconds that would have taken hours of cutting and pasting from StackOverflow.

But I am sounding cynical, the reality is that ChatGPT is like a calculator handed to someone who has only had a book of logarithms and a slide ruler until now. It is better at digesting search results than traditional means and the world has changed as a result—just as with that calculator.

And more change is certainly coming. Billions of dollars are being thrown at generative language models, and by the time you read this, who knows what will have happened.

---

[8] At some point my mother must have noticed I was using a whole bottle of triple sec, right?

My point is this: everything in this book where I talk about tech and data for Compliance holds the same as when I wrote it. The difference is that now it is more achievable than ever. If you have a tech company with skills in transformers linked with knowledge graphs and skills at scraping laws from the web, give me a call!

For everyone else, just replace "Google for Compliance" with "ChatGPT for Compliance" or "Fanciest New Thing For Compliance."

At this point we have solved improving the pillars of Compliance, but there's a gap, a big one, between where any given bank is today and the nicely linked boxes in my little diagram depicted earlier. And I've also omitted a dark truth: for many companies it may be impossible to ever fully achieve putting in all the arrows from the picture.

Why potentially impossible? Because every business group has a slightly different process, with different systems and different words (taxonomies) they use. The standard solution, including the one I detailed previously, is a new global process, system, and standard taxonomy. But a global solution, by definition, can't and won't cope with business-specific needs. For example, maybe the procedure for the mortgage business aren't Microsoft Word documents, but instead online help screens in the bank's mortgage systems. And that system might be made by a software vendor who doesn't provide any way to bidirectionally link those screens to the company's law database.

It's deeper than that though. Businesses need their own compliance systems that vary based on the products, markets, and kinds of customers. For example, a client onboarding system that has checks for KYC—in order to prevent money laundering—will collect different data for: consumer mortgages in New Hampshire; an international hedge fund with high-net worth customers;[9] industrial financing for vehicle fleet leases.

At the same time, the larger corporate entity needs data to be harmonized from these multiple systems to evaluate the compliance risk across the company, such as the KYC risk, but also all other risks: privacy, disclosures, trade reporting, insider trading, and so on. Harmonizing

---

[9] Industry jargon for "Money McMoneybags," which is generally frowned upon as a term.

requires translating terminology from the local business to corporate. For example, all the following might be equivalent for KYC, "client," "customer," "corporate entity," "consumer," "lessee," and "trust fund," but not equivalent for privacy risk.

If you mandate a single, global system, employees compensate by putting needed data that doesn't "fit" into spreadsheets or other offline documents. The new platform ends up being used only for reporting, not to operate in. The new system becomes out of date and inconsistent, requiring quality control teams to be stood up, and consultants to be massed. And then the cycle repeats with a different software platform. This is the primary reason the current GRC systems, that we discussed earlier in this book, fail.

Another challenge is that no company stands still, and no technology is forever. Systems grow old and are pushed to the side. Companies are bought and sold and their systems come along for the ride, only to be merged or ousted like an in-laws casserole at a newlyweds Thanksgiving.[10]

Even if we did mandate that one system to replace all the existing, or at least fewer systems,[11] we still need to find all the procedures, controls, and so on, extract them from the current home, load them into the new system, and then figure out which ones link to which laws. Doing that will be expensive and take a very long time—so long a time that management will likely be rotated out during the project and the work will be abandoned. I say this having witnessed it more often than not. Actually I've only ever seen it fail.

The solution is to separate the ability to work with data in the way we want from having to have that data in a single system. This bridge from today's mess to get the connected, linked data we need what I call "Google for Compliance"—because having a catchy slogan always helps when trying to maintain the attention of management. It's also true.

---

[10] That has not happened to me. I make a very nice salt and pepper noodle kugle that everyone loves.

[11] One bank I know had more than two dozen risk and compliance systems across the company.

Search can let us have one, two, or as many systems as the business needs while being able to support Compliance as if we had only one.

This is precisely what search, and therefore Google, does for us on the Internet. Every company has their own servers, data, applications, and within our browser we can view it all as a unified ocean to surf. We can query "pizza" and be offered a dozen places to order one from, methods of making, and that it is worth 25 points in Scrabble.

Google does this by developing a "knowledge graph" across all the sites it crawls where it can intuit what we mean by "pizza" and what might want to do with one (order, make, use for a triple word score). This knowledge graph is a technology approach of linking data based on user actions, machine learning, and expert knowledge. It lets us integrate knowledge without having to change existing systems.

Here's what a knowledge graph might look like, per Wikipedia:

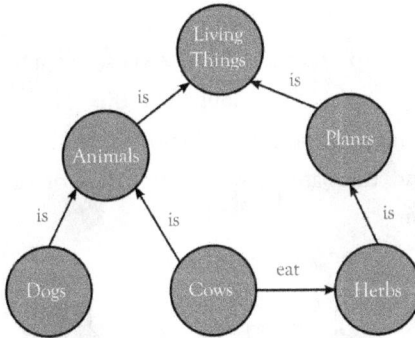

For the bank, replace the terms depicted in the picture with "loan," "mortgage," "credit," "account," and so on. And yes, I could have done that. But I didn't, and I have no excuse. Moving on.

An Example Use Case

We talked back in *So What Does Compliance Really Do?* about the regulator asking a bank how it was handling regulations related to font size, aka font size, and that to answer it would require a lot of e-mailing and cutting and pasting. The picture looked like this:

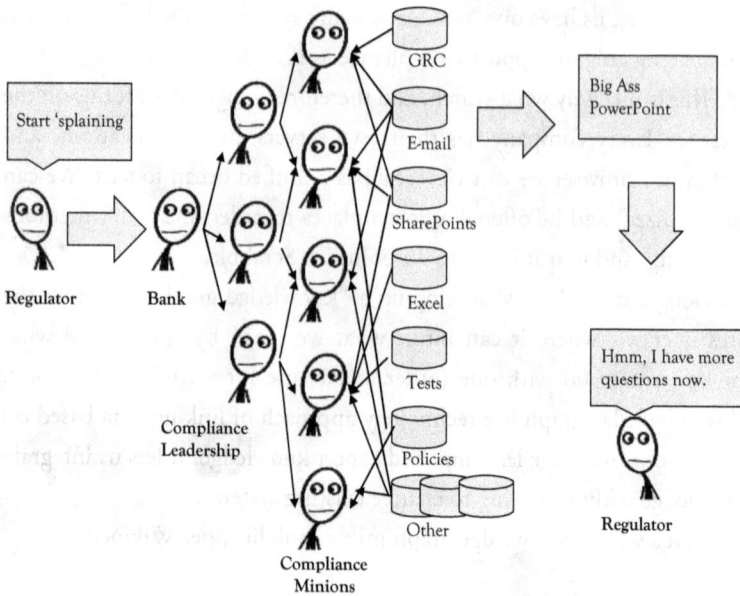

Instead, we want to link these systems via search and take the people out of the finding process. That looks like this. Here the lines are the search engine connecting across databases using the knowledge graph to understand and translate between the patois of each business and corporate function.

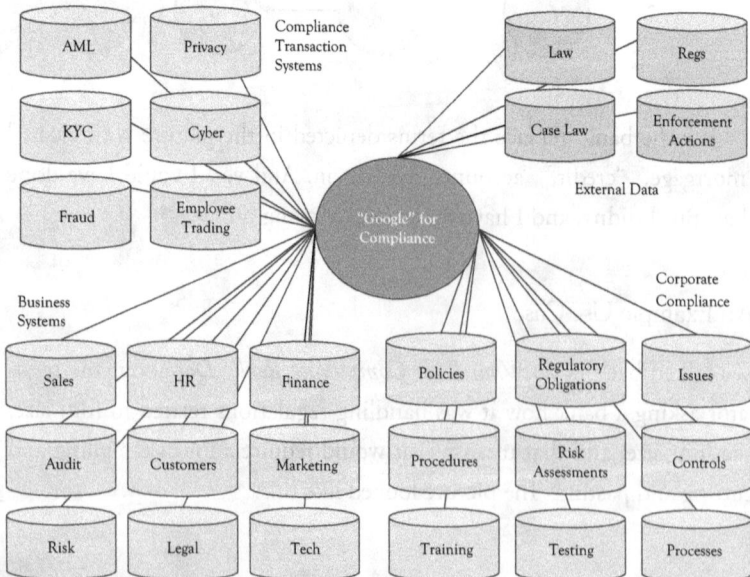

Can I Have It?

In a word: maybe. There are technical challenges. The nature and struc-ture of the Internet allows Google to do its thing, and there are significant differences with the way corporate information works.

For the most popular topics on the Internet there are billions of doc-uments, millions of users, and thousands of searches every second. These documents are also linked together with the most relevant documents having the most links to them. This is the heart of Google's Page Rank algorithm that got them started originally. Relevance is provided by the social fabric of the Internet.

Contrast this with corporate information. In a company, there are maybe hundreds of documents and a few dozen users for a given topic with a handful of searches a month. And, crucially, there aren't links between the various systems. I mean, that's what we're trying to build in the previous picture because it doesn't exist naturally!

For this reason, most companies have given up on the Google search appliance—Google's attempt to break into intranet search. It doesn't work with the way corporate data is created and maintained.

But there is a way in which the procedures, issues, tests, and financial data are better than the Internet. On the web, no individual piece of information is trustworthy. I could post on Twitter that Kim Kardashian has begun another round of missile tests over South Korea. This is not the right Kim, and Google will know this because of the weight of evidence to the contrary.

By contrast, my internal data at the bank is all true. Or at least "true" in the sense that no one is making a fake corporate procedure document.[12] The domain of the data is also much smaller than the entire World Wide Web. Given this truth, and scale, we can build a knowledge graph off of less data.

There is some work that has been done in this space and some banks and software companies that have made progress. I fully expect more and better solutions to emerge over the course of time. I also have a lot more

---

[12] Yes, of course, maybe. And in the cases of fraud, possibly. But fraudsters are lazy too and they are more likely just ignoring corporate documents rather than inventing them. Keeping two sets of books is a lot of effort—easier just to pay off the auditors.

specific thoughts on how to implement, how to translate other Google stuff like A/B testing to the corporate world, but that's beyond the scope of this book. Or, put another way, I am available if you want to make this. I charge by the hour.

Thesis 4. Effective External Oversight

Make regulatory oversight effective with meaningful penalties and external oversight.

Lastly, we need to fix the regulatory system—as if asking banks to change in the previous three thesis wasn't Herculean enough—now I want to make government change? Well, we have to. The incentive to enact those earlier changes is only going to happen if regulators demand it. But they must demand something more than just financial penalties.

When talking about how to reorganize Compliance I suggested that it is very similar to Audit—from a governance standpoint a certified valid financial statement is fundamental in the same vein as documentation that we are in compliance with the law. We can extend from here into the ways sound auditing practices are promulgated.

Generally Accepted Compliance Standards

Auditors have standards. I don't mean that they won't eat a hot dog that fell on the floor for more than 10 seconds. I can't speak to that. Maybe I should have had lunch before I wrote this paragraph. *Ahem.* There are international standards, notably the *International Financial Reporting Standards*. In the United States, we have the Financial Accounting Standards Board that issues *Generally Accepted Accounting Standards*.[13] While these two have differences, the main point is that if you are going to keep track of money, there's an accepted way to do it.

Compliance, as noted, has some wishy–washy "pillars" that nobody agrees on, or even how many pillars there are. We instead need strong standards that are set by an independent body. This probably can't be any

---

[13] Of course, like baseball's World Series that doesn't include the world outside the United States, "generally accepted" here, means the same thing.

of the existing groups, such as FINRA, Nacha, CME, and so on because each focuses only on part of the financial market.

I recommend setting up a new organization, funded by the corporations, to make and drive standards. There is, of course, compliance outside of banking, so funding of this new group need not be limited to financial firms. It's probably better to include other industries from the start, such as technology, healthcare, aerospace, pharmaceutical, and so on.

Technology companies could well be the best placed to take leadership here. Regulatory activity against Meta, Google, Microsoft, Amazon, Apple, and so on has been on the increase. Those firms are known for finding better ways to do things, and would therefore have both the impetus and capability to take leadership here. Banks, always fearful of too much change too fast, could come along for the ride.

External Compliance Certification

Continuing the analogy to Audit, standards might give management confidence in their accounting team, but nobody on the outside trusts a company to deliver the unvarnished financial truth without an external audit.[14] If you are a public company, or you want to sell your company, or you have private investment, or you just want good governance, you need externally audited and certified financials. We need auditors to do Compliance certification also—specifically to those standards proposed earlier.[15]

Going a step further, there's a potential for this external auditing to lead to other, related, outsourced Compliance services. For example, companies struggle to build Finance departments because of the cost and complexity. They therefore turn to external experts for payroll, tax, treasure, and so on. This is, as we have seen, also very true of Compliance—see

---

[14] Yes, external auditing firms are far from perfect—Enron, Madoff, Worldcom, and so on. But they are still much better in the majority of cases than not having them at all. You could actually say that these scandals have improved auditing oversight—although I honestly can't tell if they did.

[15] To anyone reading this from Accenture, Deloitte, KPMG, Ernst and Young, PwC, and so on, feel free to call me to get in on the ground floor.

earlier about smaller firms trying to hire staff who know literally all the regs for less salary than a law school graduate.

Outsourced Compliance could, in turn, reinforce the standards and external auditing that gave rise to the demand for such. A virtuous circle of increasing professionalism in Compliance.

A Penalty That Matters

Current penalties are backward looking, too small to matter, and focused on "bad apples." What gets the C-suite to pay attention is limitations on the business: no new acquisitions or a cap on assets have been used before. I propose something even stronger, no new customers for a business line until it passes regulatory review. Mortgages run deceptively? No new mortgages. Credit card fees bait and switch? No new cards. International money laundering? No cross-border transactions till you prove you aren't moving drug lord profits.

Imagine a world where you walk in a bank branch and they say:

> Sorry, we can't open an account for you because we are not in compliance with the law. But we're working on it, give us a few years and let us go through a few rounds of hiring and firing our Compliance staff, OK? In the meantime, would you like a lollipop? They rot your teeth, but we aren't responsible for that.

I suspect Compliance might start mattering once it really affects the bottom line. And if and when that happens, please consider items 1 to 9 to get you there a little faster and with some less round robining of Compliance staff.

CHAPTER 7

The End

When I was a child I had a book called, *The Monster at the End of This Book, Starring Grover*. In a very meta fashion, Grover, a blue puppet from Sesame Street without a diabetic cookie disorder, reads the title and announces that if you don't turn any pages, we won't get to the monster.

The book proceeds with Grover attempting to hold you back advancing the pages by building fences and walls and tying pages together with rope. Of course this doesn't work, the walls are drawings on paper—there were no virtual reality headsets in the 1970s. By the end, Grover is surrounded by rumble of the destroyed barricades and resigns himself to meeting the monster at the end of the book. It does seem hopeless and he gives in.

But then the twist! Grover is a monster himself and he is the monster at the end of the book. So silly of us to have been worried. And so it is here. After pages and pages of despair at the monster of criminal activity, we come here to the end. The monster is all of us. Either directly fudging edges of legality or dragged along because of our own feelings of the helplessness of fighting the system.

My hope is that you have arrived here and have learned something that might be akin to Grover's epiphany. If we accept that the monster is inside all of us, and that we don't want that for ourselves, our friends, or our society, we can change. Perhaps, this is Pollyannaish, but at heart, I am not a cynic. I believe we can do better. Banks can be trustworthy. Compliance can reduce financial crime. And we can, if we want, as I suggest in my title, stop harming customers.

Glossary

A curated set of terms you may not know and therefore want the definition of. Curated in the sense that I picked some I felt like writing about. Definition in the sense of, you may end up wanting to Google anyway. Also, I make no promises that I haven't copied from something I said in the text. Or not.

Enforcement Action: When a regulatory gives a bank a financial penalty or sends a miscreant to jail. The former is far more common than the latter. You have to really p@#$ off the government by doing so publicly offensive to get jail. Bernie Madoff, Jeff Skilling, and Martha Stewart are examples of that kind of behavior. If you're going to steal money, try not to have a media presence before or after.

MRA, Matter Requiring Attention: The regulator asks you nicely, in a letter, to fix something. The MRA is confidential because friends don't let friends air their dirty laundry.

MRIA, Matter Requiring Immediate Attention: The regulator asks you to please fix something, and you've got 30 days or some other limited amount of time before they stop being friendly about it. Just like an MRA though, it's kept confidential between the bank and the regulator. BFFs forever.

Consent Order: A public shaming. The regulator asked you nicely, and then not nicely and now they're not happy and they are going to throw your clothes and collection of rare disco vinyl LPs out on the street for everyone passing by to see. You officially suck and you better come up with a plan to fix all this mess you made. There will also be fines. Lots and lots of fines. When you finally get your act together, the consent order will be "lifted," but the consent order on the regulator's website, like a tattoo of your favorite anime character, is never going away.

AML, Anti-Money Laundering Rules: Not to be confused with antimony, a silvery metal whose name translates as "monk killer." It is also not, sadly, like antimatter, which would imply something that annihilates into pure energy on contact with cash. Instead, it is simply the rules for preventing illegal enterprises such as drug dealers, arms dealers, and other scofflaws from turning their dirty money into clean.

AML penalties are also often the most severe—because, you see, that's the government's revenue you haven't been paying when you sold all those drugs tax free. And whatever law you broke, tax evasion is the most unforgivable.

BSA, The Bank Secrecy Act: This is the technical name for AML regulations in the United States. It has all of the things you need to know, like the fact that violating it has civil *and* criminal penalties. Meaning you can go to jail for AML violations.

KYC, Know Your Customer: These are part of AML where you need to document exactly who is opening the bank account and how you know they are who they say they are. Wearing a fake mustache and carrying a suitcase full of cash to the branch when opening an account are considered "red flags" and will lead to the filing of a *SAR* or suspicious activity report with the government. Most big banks file literally thousands of SARs a day. If you think that's too many for any regulator to really be able to make sense of, you are not alone.

Sanctions: There are two definitions here. The first is AML sanctions: When a government says don't send any money to someone, that someone has been sanctioned. A person, company, or whole country can be sanctioned. Typically, this is because your government thinks the sanctioned entity is a criminal. If you break sanctions as a bank you will get a fine, a big one, and maybe jail time.

The second is industry sanctions: When FINRA, the SEC, the CFTC, or some other group sanctions an individual or company for rule breaking and potentially bars them from working in some or all of the financial industry.

BSA/AML Officer: The person at the bank who owns the BSA/AML program. This person is required by law. Must report to the board of directors. In my manifesto, I recommend the chief compliance officer should report to the board of directors. What's interesting is that the law already makes the BSA/AML officer report to the board—in a way out ranking the current set up for Compliance. It also shows how seriously the government takes money laundering, as noted in the AML entry.

This is the person most likely to be personally fined or sent to jail for violations. It's a risky job to take if you think the company is not on the up and up. I get a shiver down my back when I see it, and I see it frequently, listed—along with other more mundane compliance responsibilities—in a job description for a sole contributor at a FinTech start-up or crypto company.

TL/DR, Too Long. Didn't Read: An Internet shorthand phrase. Not compliance related. I didn't know if you knew. So I put it here. Why are you still reading this?

Three Lines of Defense: The three lines of defense against the dark arts. I mean defense of the control environment of the bank. Can we go back to the dark arts? That sounds like more fun. No? OK. Line 1: The business owns the controls and the risks associated with breaking controls, including regulatory ones. Line 2: Compliance, Technology, HR, Finance, and so on, all of the functional areas of the firm are responsible for the design of the controls. Line 3: Audit. Lords it over everyone when the potions misfire and a portal to he-who-shall-not-be-named is opened up. I think that's right.

Law: Laws are made by legislatures. They are sometimes called *statutes* or *acts*. This may make you think of marble figures without arms and the parts of plays. Nothing could be more wrong. Stop thinking that. Laws can be at the level of multinational (EU), countries, states, provinces, territories, indigenous nations, counties, cities, and probably other things. Laws can be on the books, proposed, or repealed. There are a lot of laws.

Regulation: Regulations are the rules made by agencies of governments that enforce the laws. A single law can spawn precisely one zillion regulations. The gap, real or perceived, between what a law says in broad terms and what the associated agency regulation stipulates very specifically is the source of infinite law firm revenue.

Rule: A rule can be a requirement that is not regulatory, such as those made by industry bodies including FINRA, NACHA, or some other all caps entity. Or it can be a synonym for a regulation. Why? Who knows. People are difficult to understand.

Guidance: This is neither a law, nor a regulation, nor a rule. Guidance can be a few paragraphs issued by a regulator about how they tend to interpret a given regulation. It can also be dozens of pages of extremely detailed requirements all on their own, such as the *FFIEC IT Examination Handbook*, which, if printed, would be very hard to hold in your hand. Whether guidance has the force of law, is a fun topic to ask a lawyer if you have nothing better to do with your time and your train is late. It is also an amusing query for a regulator, who may give you a penalty just for asking. I recommend giving it a try sometime.

Penalty: Penalties can be civil or criminal. Civil means you pay a fine or that you are prevented from working in a bank for some period of time, or forever, or similar. Criminal means you go to jail or go on probation—I don't know what you did and am in no position to determine anyway. Read all the "or"s in this paragraph as being inclusive, in the sense of either or both, or, if you are a person who abuses grammar, think of them as "and/or"—but please don't do that. I hate it more than I hate two spaces after periods.

RCSA, Risk and Control Self-Assessment: There's a whole chapter on this. Didn't you read it? Did you skip right to the glossary? Are you just skimming the book? Go back and read the chapter. It's great stuff.

Self-Regulatory Organization: An attempt by a group of companies to get the government off their back by saying they will take care of their own. Like the Mafia, but with a website and printed rule book.

GSO, Government Sponsored: Entity with friendly sounding names like Fannie, Freddie, or ExIm Bank. They are funded by the government, but aren't the government. They make rules and enforce them, but aren't subject to the same oversight as the government. They operate in the shadows and sometimes back mortgages. People complain about the CFPB, which was created by Congress—they should really pay more attention to the GSOs.

Confidential Supervisory Information (CSI): When a regulator asks questions of a bank or tells a bank privately that they are bad people (see MRA and MRIA), this is considered confidential supervisory information. Supervisory information because it's well, information from a supervisor. Confidential because you can't tell anyone. If you do, you'll make the regulator sad, and they will fine you and maybe send you to jail. Nobody likes a sad regulator.

Supervisor: A fancy name for a regulator. Think trattoria instead of Italian-style restaurant where breadsticks are not free.

Personally Identifiable Information (PII): I don't think I used this in the book anywhere, and I'm too lazy to check. But I think it's a nice example of a stupid acronym. PII is your name, address, social security number, phone number, e-mail, and so on. It's stuff that can identify you.

Except it's not. You could give me a list of phone numbers and I wouldn't be able to figure out who the people are. It also sounds like a misplaced modifier—"information that can be identified by a person." "Hey, Larry, I just saw a PDF file. That's the fourth information I identified today! Mark it down on my scorecard."

Instead it's the stuff that you don't want to see in an e-mail from your bank that says, "500 million PII records were accidentally put on a USB stick and mailed to Santa Claus." Why not just call it personal information?

An Appendix on the Law

Did you know that in the United States the federal government publishes its own laws, but state law is published by publishers? Specifically Thomson Reuters and LexisNexis. They have contracts with the 50 states to publish and provide access. Paid access. In many cases, the access is free for individuals, but any real use such as by corporations or lawyers often requires subscription fees.

Things have gotten better with the (divided) Supreme Court ruling in *Georgia v. Public.Resource.Org* in 2020 that states can't copyright annotations to the law. Annotations being not the law, but associated judicial rulings that help you understand and interpret the law.

This all gets complicated and nuanced, too much for a little appendix to bear, but I thought you should know that the law isn't always free to read. That's the main thing. Which is weird, barely known, and awful.

An Appendix on Performance Assessment

Performance assessment as practiced in almost all corporations is, and I apologize for not being blunt enough: stupid, demeaning, cruel, and valueless.

Think about how the people you work with got hired. They went through a long and arduous interview and hiring process. Thousands of resumes were received for all their jobs and this was the person we picked. So we have a great team? Of course not! After you've been here a year, we're ready to tell you how much you suck. That makes perfect sense.

Part of the assessment process is to rate how you did this year. But why would I rate myself less than perfect? Am I knowingly doing a bad job? Yet, if I give myself perfect scores, my boss will say, "I don't agree." By that statement they mean I am supposed to go back and lower my rating of myself—because no one is perfect.

Thus, you're supposed to come up with the reasons why you're not good enough and where you can improve so that you can be judged as not being worthy of a raise or promotion. Well that's fun. Take this fork and stick it in your own eye. Nobody forced you! We just pointed out that everyone who works here has a fork they stuck in their own eye. (Except for the CEO.)

Is there a requirement that the assessments fit a bell curve distribution? Of course there isn't. I mean, that would be illegal, probably. Instead we just "notice" when a department doesn't have as many low performers as high. Or if there aren't any low performers at all. Or if there are any high performers. It's not a *curve*. That's *ridiculous*. But if you don't, we will have lots of questions for you. Lots and lots of questions.

Let's be honest, performance assessment is about providing ass-covering for the company to fire people. If you weren't perfect then there's justification to let you go. And you rated yourself! Or the boss had to step in and rate you, and we make sure the boss can't give you good marks.

I've worked at places that had another company review all the performance assessments and send them back for editing if they were too positive. We can't trust our managers to rate their employees. The managers may *like* their staff too much. That's not good.

And then we go back to daily work, always looking over our shoulder. The bosses wonder why morale is low. The company survey shows dissatisfaction with how people feel they are treated. What could it be? I know, it's those poor performers! Let's get rid of some of them, that will fix everybody up.

An Appendix on Regulations

We talked about the sheer number of banking regulations around the world, and there's no way to list them all without making this book too heavy to carry. But it is useful to get a sense of the landscape that they cover, and if you haven't seen this dystopia yet, here's the 30,000 foot flyover view with just a few of the U.S. regulators and their primary regulations.

You may be eagle eyed and note some of the regulators listed here didn't make the cut for the table of regulators in the main body of the book. This is because there's just too many!

The Federal Reserve

A: Extensions of Credit by Federal Reserve Banks

B: Equal Credit Opportunity

C: Home Mortgage Disclosure (to CFPB)

D: Reserve Requirements of Depository Institutions

E: Electronic Fund Transfers

F: Limitations on Interbank Liabilities

G: Disclosure and Reporting of CRA-Related Agreements

H: Membership of State Banking Institutions in the Federal Reserve System

I: Issue and Cancellation of Federal Reserve Bank Capital Stock

J: Collection of Checks and Other Items by Federal Reserve Banks and Funds

K: International Banking Operations

L: Management Official Interlocks

M: Consumer Leasing

N: Relations with Foreign Banks and Bankers

O: Loans to Executive Officers, Directors, and Principal Shareholders of Member Banks

P: Privacy of Consumer Information (to CFPB)

Q: Capital Adequacy of Bank Holding Companies, Savings and Loan Holding Companies, and State Member Banks

R: Exceptions for Banks from the Definition of Broker in the Securities Exchange Act of 1934

S: Reimbursement to Financial Institutions for Providing Financial Records; Recordkeeping Requirements for Certain Financial Records

T: Credit by Brokers and Dealers

U: Credit by Banks and Persons other than Brokers or Dealers for the Purpose of Purchasing or Carrying Margin Stock

V: Fair Credit Reporting

W: Transactions between Member Banks and Their Affiliates

Y: Bank Holding Companies and Change in Bank Control

Z: Truth in Lending

AA[1]: Unfair or Deceptive Acts or Practices (to CFPB)

BB: Community Reinvestment

CC: Availability of Funds and Collection of Checks

DD: Truth in Savings (Repealed)

EE: Netting Eligibility for Financial Institutions

FF: Obtaining and Using Medical Information in Connection with Credit

GG: Prohibition on Funding of Unlawful Internet Gambling

HH: Designated Financial Market Utilities

II: Debit Card Interchange Fees and Routing

JJ: Incentive-Based Compensation Arrangements

KK: Swaps Margin and Swaps Push-Out

LL: Savings and Loan Holding Companies

MM: Mutual Holding Companies

NN: Retail Foreign Exchange Transactions

OO: Securities Holding Companies

PP: Definitions Relating to Title I of the Dodd-Frank Act

QQ: Resolution Plans

RR: Credit Risk Retention

TT: Supervision and Regulation Assessments of Fees

---

[1] They ran out and had to double up.

VV: Proprietary Trading and Relationships with Covered Funds
WW: Liquidity Risk Measurement Standards
XX: Concentration Limit
YY: Enhanced Prudential Standards

Consumer Financial Protection Bureau

B: Equal Credit Opportunity Act
C: Home Mortgage Disclosure
D: Alternative Mortgage Transaction Parity
E: Electronic Fund Transfers
F: Fair Debt Collection Practices Act
G: S.A.F.E. Mortgage Licensing Act—Federal Registration of Residential Mortgage Loan Originators
H: S.A.F.E. Mortgage Licensing Act—State Compliance and Bureau Registration System
J: Land Registration
K: Land Registration
L: Special Rules of Practice
M: Consumer Leasing
P: Privacy of Consumer Financial Information
V: Fair Credit Reporting
X: Real Estate Settlement Procedures Act
Z: Truth in Lending
DD: Truth in Savings
Payday Lending Rule: Payday, Vehicle Title, and Certain High-Cost Installment Loans
Unfair, Deceptive, or Abusive Acts or Practices (UDAAP Exam Manual)

Federal Deposit Insurance Corporation

Participation in Lotteries and Related Activities
Appraisals
Minimum Security Devices and Procedures and Bank Secrecy Act Compliance

Advertisement of Membership
Unsafe and Unsound Banking Practices
Loans in Areas Having Special Flood Hazards
Consumer Protection in Sales of Insurance
Community Reinvestment
Activities of Insured State Banks and Insured Savings Associations
Annual Independent Audits and Reporting Requirements
Standards for Safety and Soundness
Real Estate Lending Standards

Federal Emergency Management Agency

National Flood Insurance Program Laws and Regulations

Federal Financial Institutions Examination Council

FFIEC HMDA Tools
FFIEC IT Exam Handbook Infobase
FFIEC BSA/AML InfoBase

Federal Trade Commission

E-Sign Act
Fair Credit Reporting Act (FCRA)
Fair Debt Collection Protection Act (FDCPA)

National Credit Union Administration

NCUA Federal Credit Union Act

Office of the Comptroller of the Currency

OCC Comptroller's Handbook[2]
Sales of Credit Life Insurance

---

[2] There are more than 90 of these "handbooks" covering everything from Agricultural Lending to Unique and Hard-to-Value Assets.

Consumer Protection in Sales of Insurance

Minimum Security Devices and Procedures, SAR & BSA Compliance Program

Loans in Areas Having Special Flood Hazards

Community Reinvestment Act (CRA)

Lending Limits

Real Estate Lending and Appraisals

Guidelines Establishing Heightened Standards for Certain Large Insured National Banks, Insured Federal Savings Associations, and Insured Federal Branches

Department of Justice

Servicemembers Civil Relief Act (SCRA)

U.S. Department of the Treasury

FinCEN Statutes and Regulations

OFAC

Rules for Banks

Securities Exchange Commission

Organization; Conduct and Ethics; and Information and Requests

Rules of Practice

Informal and Other Procedures

Rules Relating to Investigations

Rules Relating to Debt Collection

Standards of Professional Conduct for Attorneys Appearing and Practicing Before the Commission in the Representation of an Issuer

Forms Prescribed under the Commission's Rules of Practice

Form and Content of and Requirements for Financial Statements, Securities Act of 1933, Securities Exchange Act of 1934, Public Utility Holding Company Act of 1935, Investment Company Act of 1940, Investment Advisers Act of 1940, and Energy Policy and Conservation Act of 1975

Rules Governing Crowdfunding Offerings of up to $1 million

Standard Instructions for Filing Forms Under Securities Act of 1933, Securities Exchange Act of 1934 and Energy Policy and Conservation Act of 1975 Regulation S-K

Securities Act of 1933

Trust Indenture Act of 1939

Securities Exchange Act of 1934

Regulations M, SHO, ATS, AC, and NMS and Customer Margin Requirements for Security Futures

Regulation FD

Regulation G

Regulation Blackout Trading Restriction (Regulation BTR ? Blackout Trading Restriction)

Regulation R—Exemptions and Definitions Related to the Exceptions for Banks from the Definition of Broker

Regulation S-P: Privacy of Consumer Financial Information

Proprietary Trading and Certain Interests in and Relationships with Covered Funds

Investment Company Act of 1940

Investment Advisers Act of 1940

Securities Investor Protection Corporation

Financial Industry Regulatory Authority

General Standards

Member Application and Associated Person Registration

Duties and Conflicts

Supervision and Responsibilities Relating to Associated Persons

Financial and Operational Rules

Securities Offering and Trading Standards and Practices

Quotation, Order, and Transaction Reporting Facilities

Clearing, Transaction and Order Data Requirements, and Facility Charges

Investigations and Sanctions

Code of Procedure
Code of Arbitration Procedure
Uniform Practice Code
Code of Arbitration Procedure for Customer Disputes
Code of Arbitration Procedure for Industry Disputes
Code of Mediation Procedure

Apocrypha

Stuff without a home that I wrote and don't know where to put it, so I put it here for your enjoyment. Enjoy!

The Incidents

In a dark-wood-paneled room, the executives gathered. It was a smallish room with 10 leather seats. Most were the same, but some were older and wobblier. The late arrivals got those, unless they were senior executives, in which case the more junior, such as me, would jump up to relinquish a more stable seat and go take a wobbler or lean against the credenza. One window gazed over the Manhattan skyline, one wall hid a whiteboard—these were the days before Zoom would add a giant LCD to every conference. Instead, on the center of the table was a gray starfish, a Polycom speaker that allowed callers to dial in when summoned. On the remaining walls modern art. Scary modern art. A woman with an insane gaze on a field of red and purple.

Where to look in such a meeting? Not out the window, that was tantamount to falling asleep. Not at the executives, they might fling a question about what you thought of the goings on, and that would not go well. Not at the scary lady, not without losing your soul. So I looked sort of at my shoes. But not directly. Don't look anywhere directly.

There was the head of risk. A man of few smiles who would start the meeting when he opened his glasses case and end it when he closed it. I had heard he lived in California and commuted, at the company's expense, every week, staying in a luxury hotel with such regularity that they had monogrammed his sheets for him. Who knows if it was true. Who would dare ask him?

There was the head of operations, ex-military, straight of back, and squinty of eye, the head of Compliance, with a laugh as he spoke that said, "you said that? really?" and my boss, the head of Operational Risk who had, when I met her in Brooklyn for the first time, worn a denim pantsuit. Here she wore a short sleeve blue button down. Next to me was a jovial man from Risk who kept a sousaphone in his office. Before we had entered the room, he and I had stood in the executive pantry and filled paper coffee cups with free M&Ms and popcorn—a perk we did not have on our lower floors.

"I always consider these meetings a put on my career," he had said. Meaning, any meeting on this floor could be one's last at the company.

What were we there for? The operational risk incident report. All the shit that had gone wrong in the past month. There were errors made. Some in the banks favor, some in the customers favor, but they were errors nonetheless.

"The data center in Dublin had a cable cut knocking out transactions across Europe," my boss read from the report.

"How did that happen?" the Operations Head asked. "We put redundant communication cables in separate conduits in every data center."

"They both ran down the same street and the city is working on a trolley line. They cut both." A voice on the phone said. It was the Dublin business continuity leader. He had been summoned to make this call late in the evening.

"Are we checking the other data centers to see if we have this problem elsewhere?" the head of Compliance said.

"A full review," my boss said. We were? She looked at me. Oh right, we would be. I took a note.

And here's the kicker. *La pièce de résistance.* The estimated loss of the data center incident was $50 million. Which means it barely made the cut for the meeting. Only that and larger got discussed on the high floors in Manhattan. $100 million. $250 million. Anything smaller was someone lower in the organization's problem. And there was a full page of items, or more, to get through. Every month.

"Item 2," the Head of Risk said.

Next was a trade that had gone wrong when someone pushed approve when they meant to push review.

Then there was a fine from a regulator for misleading credit card disclosures.

Then there was the hacker attack that had overwhelmed the network for 15 minutes.

We were almost at the end. The cleaning cloth had been removed and was half wrapped around the Head of Risk's spectacles.

"Why are both pages numbered one?" he asked.

My boss shot me a look.

"I, um, forgot to fix it when we added the second page. I…"

He continued wrapping his glasses. "Fix it." he said.

"Yes," I said.

And the case snapped shut.

I need to set something straight here. This meeting didn't happen. A lot of meetings like this happened. I have combined characters and meeting rooms and incidents from several different firms. The fear, the undercurrent of terror, the other undercurrent of dull routine, the microscopic analysis of some details of the report and the running out of time for others.

An Aside About Page Numbers

I will say, the page number was not something idiotic to notice. This meeting would be followed by another, and another, all day long, each with 10, 20, or more pages of material laboriously produced and funneled up the organization. How could the execs know if the documents were correct? They couldn't, so they would pounce on any perceived irregularity.

To put it another way, Anthony Bourdain once said, *I won't eat in a restaurant with filthy bathrooms. This isn't a hard call. They let you see the bathrooms. If the restaurant can't be bothered to replace the puck in the urinal or keep the toilets and floors clean, then just imagine what their refrigeration and work spaces look like.* A wrong page number, a different colored box, and a wrong date, these are the dirty bathrooms of corporate PowerPoints.

About the Author

David Silverman has been an executive at banks including JPMorgan Chase, Wells Fargo, Citi, Morgan Stanley, and CIBC. He has seen firsthand how the largest financial institutions operate and worked with thousands of other Compliance officers who toil daily to protect customers. David has a BA in mathematics and computer science from Drew University and is working toward a master's in computer science from the University of Illinois at Urbana Champaign. He is the author of *Typo, The Last American Typesetter*.

Index